IDEOLOGY IN AMERICA

To Kim and Liz
in warmest friendship
boundless respect
and
the hope of peace

Alan Geyer

Also by Alan Geyer
and published by Westminster John Knox Press

with Barbara G. Green
Lines in the Sand: Justice and the Gulf War

Piety and Politics: American Protestantism in the World Arena

Ideology
IN AMERICA
Challenges to Faith

ALAN GEYER

Westminster John Knox Press
Louisville, Kentucky

Scripture quotations from the New Revised Standard Version
of the Bible are copyright © 1989 by the Division of Christian Education
of the National Council of the Churches of Christ in the U.S.A.
and are used by permission.

Book design by Jennifer K. Cox
Cover design and
illustration by Alec Bartsch

First edition
Published by Westminster John Knox Press
Louisville, Kentucky

This book is printed on acid-free paper that meets the
American National Standards Institute Z39.48 standard. ∞

PRINTED IN THE UNITED STATES OF AMERICA
97 98 99 00 01 02 03 04 05 06 — 10 9 8 7 6 5 4 3 2 1

Library of Congress Cataloging-in-Publication Data

Geyer, Alan F.
    Ideology in America : challenges to faith / Alan Geyer — 1st ed.
        p.   cm.
    Papers presented at various conferences at various places from 1967 to
1993.
    Includes bibliographical references and index.
    ISBN 0-664-25633-3 (alk. paper)
    1. Ideology—Religious Aspects—Christianity. 2. Sociology, Christian—
United States. I. Title.
BR115.I35G48 1997
261.7'0973—dc21   97-1731

TO CHRIS AND LISSIE,
young partners in my convivium

CONTENTS

PREFACE

This is a book about ideas and their functions in American political and religious life.

In many ways, both the American government and the American economy are sources of envy around the world. The endurance of the world's oldest constitution, the vitality of civil liberties, the unmatched productivity of the economy, and the affluence of a majority of the population (including millions of recent immigrants) all combine to generate national pride (with an inflated triumphalism since the end of the Cold War) and international respect (if not universal affection). All this is true.

But this book tells a different story—the story of a government and an economy that are failing tens of millions of U.S. citizens and distressing hundreds of millions of citizens of other nations. Such troubles clamor for Christian understanding and action.

The sources of failure and distress are much deeper than the responsibilities of contemporary political and economic leaders. They are rooted in the same history and culture that have produced such conspicuous success. And the responsibilities are shared by educators, journalists, and religious leaders—as well as by the citizenry.

Yet there is a particular development in the past two decades that must fix special responsibility on those political and corporate elites who have waged what I call the Regressive Revolution—the resurgence of some of the most primitive elements in the mainstream of American ideology. That resurgence has variously inspired and rationalized policies that have compounded the sufferings of marginalized peoples and impoverished the common treasuries of environment and culture. Those pragmatic politicians, technocratic academics, and above-it-all theologians of generally progressive mentality have not really figured out how to cope with the Regressive Revolution because they have remained mostly in denial of the inevitability and the positive necessities of ideology.

So this is a book about ideology—why we have troubles with it and why we cannot do without it.

As a teacher of government and political philosophy at three colleges and, latterly, of ethics and politics at Wesley Theological Seminary in Washington, I have sought to engage students in critical inquiry into most of the topics of these pages. For ten years, as director of the Churches' Center for Theology and Public Policy, I recruited scholars and policy-makers for discussion of the theology of politics and of political economy. And for many more years, my encounters with scholars and churches around the world (especially in Eastern Europe) have forced me to search carefully for both the possibilities and limits of dialogue across the ideological boundaries of the Cold War and post–Cold War chaos.

This book has been aborning for a long, long time. It had its genesis in my 1967 Raymond Walters Lectures, "Political Ethics as a Christian Discipline," at the University of Cincinnati. In a 1968 address to the Chicago Interseminary Faculties Union, I began to set forth what I called a "convivial theology," whose themes are briefly sketched in this book. In 1981, I developed some of these themes for the World Council of Churches' (WCC) Consultation on Political Ethics in Cyprus in a presentation titled "Towards an Ecumenical Political Ethics: A Marginal American View," which was subsequently published by the WCC in *Perspectives on Political Ethics*. In 1985, my presidential address for the Society of Christian Ethics, "Politics and the Ethics of History," updated my perspectives on the ways in which ideology uses and abuses the interpretation of history. In 1992, at an international seminar in Uppsala, Sweden, hosted by the Life and Peace Institute, my paper on "Politics, Power, and Human Rights" addressed some of the theological and ecumenical issues recapitulated for this book. Much of the substance of the main constructive chapter (chapter 9, after a bout of deconstruction!) was presented in an address to the 1993 annual meeting of CAREE (Christians Associated for Relationships with Eastern Europe).

But it is the Regressive Revolution and its contributions to the breakdown of American governance, especially at this millennium's end, that have spurred the completion of this book during a sabbatical granted by Wesley Seminary.

In addition to my indebtedness to numberless students, colleagues, and readers who have borne the burden of my ideas over the years, my most special appreciation is owed those who have engaged the particular themes of this book, have read at least portions of it, and have responded most helpfully and critically. It is not from ingratitude but rather to spare them any taint of the faults remaining herein that I am omitting a list of their names. But there is a special list that contains just one name, that of my wife, Barbara Green, my number one dialogue partner and critic.

The great kindness and competence of the editors at Westminster John Knox Press deserve my last grateful word.

1

THE INEVITABILITY
OF IDEOLOGY

Americans are . . . remarkably naive about the relationship of economic
to political power.
                    —Seymour Martin Lipset, quoted in Waxman, ed.,
                                          The End of Ideology Debate

Many black folk now reside in a jungle ruled by a cutthroat market morality devoid of any faith in deliverance or hope for freedom. . . . But why is
this shattering of black civil society occurring? What has led to the weak-
ening of black cultural institutions in asphalt jungles? Corporate market
institutions have contributed greatly to their collapse. . . . The primary
motivation of these institutions is to make profits, and their basic strategy
is to convince the public to consume. . . . Market calculations and cost-
benefit analyses hold sway in almost every sphere of U.S. society.
                                          —Cornel West, *Race Matters*

One of America's most sophisticated political columnists, George F.
Will, recently declared that "this is an ideological moment in America." Will regards this state of affairs as "healthy because it involves
Americans in reviewing old themes, arguments, documents and principles." Moreover, "politics without clear convictions becomes either mere
brokering of interests or a cult of personality."[1]

This book is written in firm agreement with those particular words of
George Will—even if his own political diagnoses and prescriptions amount
mostly to malpractice.

This is indeed an ideological moment in America. In truth, there are
no *non*ideological moments in America, or anywhere, at any time. But
these closing years of the second millennium are marked by an intensifi-
cation of the struggle over basic political and economic beliefs, as well as
over the self-interests that those beliefs represent—or that they camou-
flage. This struggle is increasingly bitter, although millions of Americans
remain either unaware of it or disengaged from it. It is much more than
a philosophical debate. It is a war of ideas, a time of "culture wars" and
of economic aggression. It is a multifaceted social and cultural conflict in
which the enormity of human suffering, in both the United States and
around the world, is compounded by the policies of the U.S. government
and the attitudes and lifestyles of the American people.

1

The bitterness of this conflict is partially portrayed by James Davison Hunter's widely heralded 1991 book, *Culture Wars: The Struggle to Define America,* one of the strengths of which is his attention to the pervasive religious elements in American ideology and politics.[2] But Hunter's effort to "make sense of the battles over the family, art, education, law, and politics" largely neglects the economic interests at stake in ideological conflict. For what is particularly urgent at the end of this millennium is the unmasking of the many ways in which "cultural" issues are being manipulated to serve the self-interests of economic elites at a time of severely accelerating inequalities among the American people and across the Earth. Family, art, education, and law—and religiously based moral attitudes concerning them—are peculiarly susceptible to exploitation as distracting influences from social justice and the common good.

Basic to this book is the judgment that this ideological struggle has become increasingly one-sided. Most liberal and moderate politicians seem to be operating (to repeat Will's phrase) "without clear convictions" and are indeed susceptible to the criticism that they are involved in the "mere brokering of interests." Their disavowal of any meaningful labels reduces their agendas to "pragmatism" and "incrementalism."

All too many academics of generally progressive dispositions share a similar aversion to the very word *ideology,* as well as to the principled struggle over the nation's priorities. The spirited on-campus skirmishes over "political correctness" concern mostly secondary if not trivial semantic issues and serve to divert scholarly energies from the main battles out there in the public arena.

And then there are the churches, many of whose official pronouncements tilt slightly to the left but whose moral styles tend (or pretend) to be anti-ideological and whose institutional styles tend to be antipolitical. By contrast with such unofficial Christian fronts as the Christian Coalition and the Institute on Religion and Democracy, which have fused their theology with right-wing ideology, the mainline churches have disavowed ideology. They have neatly scolded both liberalism and conservatism, leaving the presumption that the moral truth is somewhere in the safe middle of the road. They have presumed to be aloof from the ideological struggle and have thereby forfeited to the forces of predatory regression.

So the struggle is indeed one-sided. The losers are not so much the liberal-to-moderate politicians, or the professional academics, or the mainline middle-class churches. The heavy losers are the nation's children, at least one-fourth of whom are now officially "poor." The losers are persons of color facing governmental retreat on civil rights, social safety nets, and public education. The losers are inner-city neighborhoods and their cultural institutions.

The ideological conquests of the 1980s and 1990s have left the United

States with the greatest concentration of wealth and the most severe inequalities of any industrial nation. The ascendancy of corporate financial and commercial institutions in the corridors of public policy, to their greatest dominance since the 1920s, has been accompanied by the precipitate decline of public interest, consumer, labor, and peace groups. Civil society is disintegrating even as the very concept of civil society is being abused to undermine humane and effective government. The rich are indeed getting richer and the poor are getting poorer. In the 1980s and 1990s, corporate profits boomed while real wages declined. Between 1982 and 1995, the value of the New York Stock Exchange increased more than 400 percent, while the average real wage declined about 15 percent. During those same years, corporations engaged in competitive downsizing have slashed their employees' health and pension plans while rewarding their top executives with multimillion-dollar bonuses.[3]

Even more broadly, then, the losers are citizens whose health, security, cultural enrichment, and access to truth are jeopardized by this ideological warfare. Not least among the losers are the peoples of a hundred or more nations whose welfare is diminished by the ideological distortions of American power in the world.

The 1996 elections offered little hope of redressing these troubles. President Bill Clinton's efforts to position himself as a "New Democrat" by co-opting such standard Republican issues as a balanced budget, tax cuts, welfare reform, family values, and toughness on crime—thereby seeking to capture the political center—no doubt were factors in his electoral successes. But they have deprived his party, his campaigns, and his administration of a strong, clear voice on behalf of the nation's, and the world's, marginalized peoples. Two political facts especially document and symbolize this predicament: (1) President Clinton's 1996 capitulation to Republican antiwelfare legislation that ends the six-decade federal commitment to the support of poor children; and (2) the persistence of military spending at Cold War levels nearly a decade after the end of the Cold War.

Moreover, the 1996 elections perpetuated the debilitations of a divided government: one party occupying the executive branch; the other, controlling Congress. Stalemated government amounts to political anarchy in matters of critical human needs. Millions of American voters, whether or not they "split the ticket," have been persuaded that divided government is somehow more democratic than party accountability and effective majority rule. The fatuous presumption is that government-by-gridlock can do less damage even if it cannot do much good. That illusion has perverse moral and ideological consequences. Stalemated, inactive government on urgent social issues means an unending triumph for the most regressive antigovernmental ideologies and the special interests they serve. Divided government has become one of the "seven deadly D's" contributing to the breakdown of American political infrastructure (outlined in chapter 9).

This is indeed a religiously loaded ideological moment in America.

The United States is retreating from a shared national commitment to social justice and the general welfare, and the churches are being asked to pick up the pieces through charity and relief on a scale they cannot possibly produce.

The United States is also retreating from a principled commitment to global cooperation on issues of justice, peace, and ecology. Early in 1995, the fiftieth anniversary of the founding of the United Nations, Jessica Mathews wrote: "Some bad angel arranged that the United Nations' 50th anniversary, which should be the occasion for clear thinking about what kind of institution the world needs for the next 50, would be the year when the Washington vogue is U.N. bashing, slashing spending on anything foreign and . . . an indifference to America's role in the world."[4]

Much of this nation is regressing to primitive myths concerning its own history and the role of government in that history, with particular disdain for the achievements of the welfare state that began to develop in the 1930s.

Self-aggrandizing economic interests have led this retreat through the lavish funding not only of political campaigns but also of the ideological and mythological manipulation of value-shaping institutions: the media, education, and religion.

Those economic interests have succeeded in forging a new coalition, a "hegemonic bloc" composed incongruously of aggressive entrepreneurs, political elites, academic mercenaries, fundamentalist impresarios, military chauvinists, syndicated columnists, and talk-show celebrities—all preaching an "authoritarian populism" that exploits middle-class and workers' anxieties about family, economic security, race, and "traditional values."

Those economic interests have fueled a wide-ranging assault on public and higher education, reshaping curricula to accommodate business and industrial interests, promoting the values of competitive individualism (along with the rhetoric of religion, virtues, family values, and patriotism), attacking the hard-won gains of minority educators and students, and advocating "freedom of choice" voucher plans for private school alternatives (even while tightening state control of public school teachers and curricula).

Those economic interests have recruited and funded a new class of articulate theologians, philosophers, and other scholars who have aggressively rationalized those interests and who function as ideological confederates of the Religious Right.

4

The national structures of the mainline churches, both denomination-ally and ecumenically, have been prime targets of this manipulation. They have been critically degraded, defunded, demoralized, and dis-membered under the ideological assault. They now have a gravely weak-ened capacity to influence public debate and decisions on social and in-ternational issues.

Yet the American churches, in the aggregate, remain the richest churches in the richest nation in the world. This is the heyday of the church-growth movement, megachurches with thousands of members, a booming market for all kinds of religious goods, and a massive religious presence in the nation's increasingly sovereign broadcast media, televi-sion and talk-radio. The disconnection between religious trends and the despair of millions of disinherited people has seldom if ever been more blatant.

The weight of religious (and political) sentiment in America today is in-creasingly antigovernmental, antiwelfare, antiurban, indifferent to racial injustice, vengeful in criminal justice, preoccupied with the divisive issues of sexuality, and disengaged from the troubles of the outside world.

It is all too true—but not very illuminating—to declare that America is in deep spiritual and moral crisis. The most progressive, the most middle-of-the-road, and the most reactionary preachers and pundits can all agree on that lamentation. But that is a meaningless lamentation unless the very definitions of spirituality and morality are included in the rhetoric.

That word *spiritual* is one of the most troublesome and seductive words in the religious vocabulary. We must handle it with great care lest it become the sanctification of the status quo, a pious excuse for oppres-sion, or a cheapening of the grace of the whole gospel. For after all, to be spiritual is to have one's heart and mind transformed for a life of love-in-action.

I will never forget a spirit-filled sermon by a gracious and courageous Southern Presbyterian preacher, the late Wellford Hobbie, to a Virginia congregation during the most intense civil rights conflicts of the 1960s. Hobbie's strange topic was "The Great Heresy of the Spirituality of the Church." What he plainly rejected was the invocation of the words *spir-itual* and *spirituality* to keep controversy out of the church, to keep the church out of politics, and therefore to keep the church in tacit support of racial segregation. Hobbie subsequently went to Selma to march with Martin Luther King, Jr.—then returned to face a painfully divided con-gregation in an open public forum to explain again why he had gone to Selma, to testify movingly but modestly about that experience, and to in-vite questions and criticisms from his listeners. Altogether, Wellford Hob-bie's words and actions provided one of the most disarmingly effective ministries of reconciliation in my experience.

Spirituality that is unconnected to the active struggle for social justice and world peace risks becoming either a private luxury or a public abuse of power and privilege.

Morality that is fixated on the presumed do's and don'ts of personal virtue, as in sexual conduct, to the neglect of society's "principalities and powers" too easily becomes a fig leaf for economic interests and covert racism.

In short, if spirituality and morality do not participate radically in what Paul called being "transformed by the renewing of your minds, so that you may discern what is the will of God" (Rom. 12:2), they are reduced to being what Paul, in another place, called "noisy gongs and clanging cymbals" (1 Cor. 13:1).

The proper and necessary work of ideology involves the renewing of the mind in matters political, social, and economic so that we may better discern the will of God.

All our value-shaping institutions, including the churches, share a responsibility to confront the inevitability of ideology and to empower people with the capacity to formulate and articulate political, social, and economic beliefs.

The process of ideological renewal must include a positive vision of the national government's moral authority and commitment to the general welfare, as well as an enduring articulation of the meaning of "liberty and justice for all." It must not simply wallow in antigovernment rhetoric or the sentimentalities of individualism. And it must embrace a vision of the moral bonds among all the earth's nations and peoples.

If Christians are able to overcome the pernicious fallacy that our faith must be kept separate from our politics, then these imperatives of ideological renewal require theological expression. They also require translation into interfaith language and secular visions in our exceedingly pluralistic society. The churches' participation in this process calls for a *political ecclesiology,* a vision of the churches' mission in the political arena that is both theologically faithful and constitutionally legitimate. In conclusion:

1. Ideology, defined as *a set of beliefs and symbols that serve to interpret social reality and motivate political action,* is both inevitable and necessary in any society.

2. Too many Americans regard *ideology* as simply a bad word and believe themselves and this nation to be either free of ideology, or needing to become so.

3. However, most Americans share a similar set of basic beliefs about government and society and economy. They in fact

share an ideology without naming it as such—an ideology that is increasingly being exploited for reactionary purposes, including the demolition of the churches' social and ecumenical ministries.

4. The churches of America are now engaged in an unprecedentedly bitter struggle with the "principalities and powers" of American politics and economic life, and with militant false prophets within the churches themselves.

5. This is unquestionably a spiritual and moral struggle, but the very definitions of *spiritual* and *moral* too often tend to be captive to narrow ideological viewpoints and to particular social and economic interests.

6. The Christian churches' mission for justice and peace requires both the discernment of the actual ideologies held by the people and the reconstruction of ideologies so that they are more responsive to the will of God for the structures of society and the world.

2

THE IDEA OF IDEOLOGY

The ideas of economists and political philosophers, both when they are right and when they are wrong, are more powerful than is commonly understood. Indeed, the world is ruled by little else. Practical men, who believe themselves to be quite exempt from any intellectual influences, are usually the slaves of some defunct economist.

—John Maynard Keynes,
The General Theory of Employment, Interest, and Money

The end of ideology, if it is in fact taking place, is a catastrophe.
—Michael Harrington, quoted in Waxman, ed.,
The End of Ideology Debate

Ideology is inevitable. Ideology is imperative. An ethic without an ideology is impossible. A theology without an ideology is impossible. Ideology is here to stay. It is in our nature as human beings and political animals. Politics that pretends to be without ideology is indeed pretentious—or self-deluded. Ideology is conspicuously endemic to industrial societies that have everywhere been marked by mass education, mass communications, mass politicization, and vast agglomerations of political and economic power.

Everybody has an ideology. It may be subconscious, unreflective, inarticulate; but everybody has some mental construct of social reality that has political implications.

The real questions are the following:

> Do you know you have an ideology? If so, do you acknowledge it?
>
> Is your ideology conscious, or do you suspect it is unconscious?
>
> Have you ever sat down and consciously thought through, in a systematic way, what you do believe or would like to believe about government and its role in society? If so, have you made a special effort to reflect on your political and economic beliefs in the light of your religious faith?

In a variety of courses at both undergraduate and graduate levels, I have required students to develop statements of their own ideologies.

Some students try to deny that they have an ideology. Others are extremely uncomfortable in thinking about it, much more so in talking about it. Some would find it easier to talk about their sex lives than their political and economic beliefs.

I have had similar experiences in local congregations, among denominational and ecumenical leaders, even among otherwise sophisticated scholars. Many Americans find it extremely difficult to come out of their ideological closets. Yet it should be the vital strength of a civil society in a self-proclaimed democracy that its citizens are self-conscious and articulate about their social and political beliefs and that they engage one another in public forums that encourage and facilitate the expression of those beliefs. The churches should not be the last places to offer such forums. Perhaps they should be the first—at least for Christians.

All of which leads again to the definition of ideology presumed in this book. *An ideology is a set of beliefs and symbols that serve to interpret social reality and motivate political action.*

An ideology may or may not be systematic, or consistent, or simplistic. It may be irenic or vicious, oppressive or redemptive.

There is a double-edged character to an ideology: It is both descriptive and normative, both interpretative and motivative. It tells us how to perceive *what is* and how to decide *what ought to be*. It provides both an empirical and a moral framework—a way of looking at both facts and values. Ideology gives content to political culture by shaping popular and personal identity and by defining political traditions and goals.

Of course, an ideology may badly distort empirical reality. Certainly, an ideology may appeal to a morality that is either vicious or naive. All too often, an ideology has become an idolatry. Some examples of ideology as idolatry are these:

> *Christendom*—when the imperial nations of Europe presupposed a Christian culture within their borders and dominated the world through their colonial empires.
>
> *Manifest Destiny*—when the continental expansiveness of white Americans conquered Native Americans and Spanish and Mexican territories.
>
> *National Socialism*—when the totalitarian tyranny and brutality of Hitler's Nazi credo captured the loyalty of the German people, including a majority of German churches.
>
> *Marxism-Leninism*—when the legitimate revolutionary grievances of the proletariat came to rationalize Russian imperialism, Stalinist terror, and international subversion.
>
> *Christian Economics*—when an ultraconservative brand of

"Christian" thought was fused with a primitive brand of laissez-faire capitalism.

Nuclear Deterrence—when the production, deployment, and possible use of nuclear weapons became the unquestionable U.S. dogma of national security, with considerable support from some theologians and the churches.

Such pernicious combinations of religious or mystical or moral claims with self-aggrandizing national or racial or class interests exhibit ideologies at their worst. And the twentieth century has surely witnessed ideologies at their worst.

So the case has to be made for ideologies at their best. Can an ideology open us up to new and more truthful perspectives on reality? Can it deepen our ethical sensitivities? Can it hold our political loyalties under the judgment of our ultimate religious loyalties? Can it equip us to engage other ideologies with respect for whatever truths they may hold? Can it empower us for sustained action in the struggle for justice and peace?

The Politics in All Theologies

This book attempts to answer "yes" to just such questions, but not before a more careful inquiry into the phenomena of ideologies. In 1962, in the midst of the most intense controversy over the original "end of ideology" pronouncements, Robert Haber irenically noted that ideology

> need not be doctrinaire, it need not be demagogic; it need not be dehumanizing of either its [advocates] or its antagonists. It need not advocate violent revolution or sacrificing of the present for the future. . . . For instance, none of these attributes apply to the nonviolent civil rights movements in the United States, yet they possess in varying degrees all the defining features of ideology and ideological politics.[1]

That a religiously inspired movement like the civil rights movement should articulate an ideology must not only dispose us to see the prophetic possibilities of an ideology, but must also move us to ask whether any religious movement or theological camp is or has ever been devoid of an ideology. Where in the world has there ever been a theology without an explicit or implicit set of beliefs and symbols that serve to interpret social reality and to motivate political action?

An assumption of this book is that every major *theological* development has had a distinctive *political* context, motive, and message. Theology does not develop in a historical vacuum. Theology itself tends to be polemical—a reaction against other patterns of thought and/or institutions judged to be wrongheaded.

This assumption bears exemplification in the dominant theological orientations of Christian history, with important implications for political thought. We may call Augustine, Aquinas, Luther, and Calvin the "Big Four" theologians of politics between the Church Fathers and the emergence of the modern nation-state system in the sixteenth and seventeenth centuries. Each addressed a particular political situation with a particular purpose and message. To be sure, each of these four was also a comprehensive theologian who addressed the whole range of basic Christian doctrine and attempted to ground his view of politics in basic doctrine. But there was a strong Pauline view of authority in each of them.

In the late fourth and early fifth centuries, Augustine sought to absolve Christianity from responsibility for the decline of the Roman Empire. In the thirteenth century, Aquinas sought to hold all the political systems of the world together in a great medieval synthesis dominated by the church and rationalized by Christian theology.

In the sixteenth century, Luther sought to free the princes of Europe from the tyranny and corruption of Roman imperialism and to give them legitimate authority at a time of emerging nationalism. And in that same century, Calvin sought to provide a body of doctrine for subordinating civil government to the teachings and counsels of his church.

Each of these "Big Four" gave priority to *order* over *justice*—thus raising the persistent question of the relation of "classical" Christian theology to democratic political thought. Democratic thought, in its most authentic versions, gives priority to *justice* over *order*, which is to say that none of the four offers a political theology in which human rights are conceived prior to political authority.

In these days when, in some Christian circles, it is fashionable to bash the eighteenth-century Enlightenment at every opportunity, it must be recalled that the philosophy, the ethics, and ultimately the contemporary theologies of human rights owe much to Locke, Montesquieu, and Jefferson—who, in turn, owe much to pre-Christian thinkers in Greece and Rome. (That eighteenth-century notions of human rights need to be expanded to do justice to contemporary economic and social realities is a main theme of chapter 9.)

Argentine theologian José Miguez Bonino, a former president of the World Council of Churches, plainly addressed this problematical theological legacy of the "Big Four" in a chapter titled "Justice and Order" in his book *Toward a Christian Political Ethics*. With regard to Augustine, Miguez Bonino observed that "justice and love are the two foundations of the eternal city that impinge on the earthly one." However, for Augustine the correction of injustices cannot be permitted to endanger "order and peace. But if any redress of wrong threatens to become disruptive, it should be avoided." "Peace" is really understood as *order*. For Augustine, "the chief purpose of societal organization is the suppression of conflict and tumult. Changes, or the respect for personal freedom or for justice, might endanger that order. . . . Theologically, justice and love are supreme, but historically both are subordinated to order."[2]

Every major theological movement of the twentieth century has also disclosed a distinctive political motive and message—which is not necessarily to discount its integrity, unless one assumes that any political connection inevitably degrades theology. The theology of crisis associated with Karl Barth, the Christian realism of Reinhold Niebuhr, the radical discipleship of Dietrich Bonhoeffer, theologies of hope and liberation, recent ecological theologies—all are forms of political theology, whether or not they claim the label.

Origins and Development
of the Idea of Ideology

While ideology has already been described as an inevitable accompaniment of any society or of any theology, the concept of ideology has a distinctly modern history. Three uniquely modern phenomena set the stage for self-conscious ideologies: nationalism, the Enlightenment, and the Industrial Revolution. The social transformations unleashed by these forces invited more systematic analyses, both of social institutions and of the ideas that shaped and were shaped by those institutions.

The term *ideology* right now is having its two-hundredth anniversary. In 1797, in the late years of the French Enlightenment, a philosopher named Antoine Destutt de Tracy coined the term. What de Tracy originally meant by ideology was simply "the science of ideas." He promoted the "rational investigation of the origin of ideas," especially in terms of common human needs and desires. Thus ideology was conceived as a natural and necessary aspect of social life. Even more, ideology offered a new science that could provide a foundation for social progress and enlightened legislation. De Tracy's systematic exposition of this new science was written between 1801 and 1815 and published under the title *Éléments d'Idéologie.*

In the century after de Tracy, the concept of ideology swung back and forth between positive and pejorative connotations. Napoleon, originally a patron of the circle of Enlightenment philosophers that included de Tracy, came to regard "ideologues" as his enemies, as the French Republic moved aggressively toward an empire bolstered by the clerical Catholic establishment. The "ideologues" were the liberal social and philosophical critics of Napoleonic aggrandizement and authoritarianism. In the process, religion and ideology were so polarized that they were regarded as incompatible and mutually exclusive. Napoleon went so far as to blame the "ideologues" for all his defeats following his disastrous retreat from Moscow: "It is to ideology, this cloudy metaphysics . . . [of] subtly searching for first causes, . . . that we must attribute all the misfortunes of our fair France."[3]

Nearly two centuries ago, then, the problematical relationships between Christianity and ideology were projected on the generations to come. Provisionally, we may suggest three alternative patterns:

1. *Religion and ideology are antithetical.* From a religious stance, ideology may be judged as perverse and inevitably idolatrous. Contrariwise, from a secular ideological base, religion may be regarded as strictly escapist or the rationalization of oppression.

2. *Religion and ideology are integral.* In this pattern, the normative principles of religion may be identified more or less absolutely with a particular set of social, political, and/or economic beliefs—as in "the Protestant ethic" (as depicted by Max Weber in *The Protestant Ethic and the Spirit of Capitalism*) or "Christian Socialism" (as endorsed by some early social gospelers and the Fellowship of Socialist Christians in the 1930s).

3. *Religion and ideology are dialectically related.* It is possible to be a partisan of a particular ideology while viewing it as subject to radical criticism in the light of Christian faith—even while also viewing theology and the life of the church as legitimately subject to radical criticism from an ideological perspective. Such a dialectical approach has been characteristic of the later Reinhold Niebuhr, John C. Bennett, J. Philip Wogaman, and a variety of Latin, feminist, and African-American theologians.

Back in the nineteenth century, it was the Marxists who had most to say about the meaning and functions of ideologies. For Karl Marx himself, ideology was essentially a negative concept that explained the rationalization of bourgeois-capitalist class interests and their narcotic religious justification. It was the concept that unmasked those interests. For Marx and his chief collaborator, Friedrich Engels, ideology was associated with the notion of a "false consciousness" that disoriented its adherents from viewing society realistically.

Vladimir Lenin deviated from Marx and Engels in attributing positive normative functions to some ideologies. In his tract *What Is to Be Done?*

Lenin declared that "the only choice is—either bourgeois or socialist ideology."[4] While Lenin was brutally intolerant of alternatives to his version of socialism, he restored the concept of ideology to Antoine Destutt de Tracy's potentially positive, functional approach. Embracing such a positive approach, the Italian Marxist Antonio Gramsci observed that "the bad sense of the word [ideology] has become widespread" and has "denatured" the further development of the concept. Gramsci was particularly attentive to the ideological functions of religion in producing "a unity of faith" between a worldview and a corresponding system of ethics.[5]

Ideology and Utopia

Perhaps the most comprehensive and constructive elaboration of the concept and functions of ideology came from Karl Mannheim's 1929 work, *Ideology and Utopia*. Eighty years after *The Communist Manifesto* was promulgated amid the social revolutions of the late 1840s, Mannheim addressed the subject of ideology amid the social and political chaos of Germany's Weimar Republic and the impending worldwide Depression. Mannheim took the Marxists to task for their uncritical absolutism about their own ideas while interpreting their opponents' ideas as mere functions of their economic and social locations.

Ideology and Utopia distinguished between "particular" and "total" conceptions of ideology. The particular conception refers to "more or less conscious disguises of the real nature of a situation, the true recognition of which would not be in accord with one's own interests." It is this capacity for deception, and even for self-deception, that marks particular ideologies. But Mannheim went beyond that to a more objective, more fundamental, and less pejorative approach.

> [He moved toward a] total conception of ideology, according to which the thought of all parties in all epochs is of an ideological character. There is scarcely a single intellectual position, and Marxism furnishes no exception to this rule, which has not changed through history and which even in the present does not appear in many forms.[6]

For Mannheim, this total conception of ideology ultimately is elaborated into the foundations of a "sociology of knowledge"—a broad, critical, yet constructive approach to the study of intellectual and social history. He did not claim special privilege for his own ideas. In a passage of enduring grace in the face of bitter ideological hostilities, he wrote: "The general form of the total conception of ideology is being used by the analyst when he has the courage to subject not just the adversary's point of view but all points of view, including his own, to the ideological analysis."[7] So Mannheim believed that philosophical commitment and ideological dialogue could be combined under a mandate of ethical integrity.

One other fruit of Mannheim's approach is of special ethical and even theological significance, and is timely for the ideological predicament addressed in these pages. Just as he served to legitimize ideology as a natural and potentially constructive category of political analysis, so Mannheim rescued *utopia* from its typically negative connotations at the hands of self-styled "political realists."

Mannheim's conception of utopia is much broader and more historically grounded than the literary fantasies of an ideal commonwealth, such as Thomas More's *Utopia*. For Mannheim, utopia refers to ideas whose orientation "transcends reality," even while "they pass over into conduct [and] tend to shatter, either partially or wholly, the order of things prevailing at the time."[8] To be sure, ideologies also are "transcendent ideas which never succeed *de facto* in the realization of their projected contents."[9] Determining what is ideological as contrasted with what is utopian, Mannheim acknowledged, is exceedingly problematical in any given historical moment. In fact, he was not entirely consistent in his interpretations of ideology. (At times, the pejorative connotations led him to prefer "point of view" or "perspective.") But in places, he saw utopia as the realizable vision of a future society, in contrast with ideology as the idealized conceit of society's dominant or ascendant classes. Such a distinction leaves open to historians the judgment as to what beliefs actually functioned as utopias and which ones functioned as ideologies.

Given that potential for confusion, it may make more sense, at least for Christians struggling with social and political ideas, to view utopias as imaginative forms of ideology rather than as an entirely different class of thought.

A utopia, then, is a vision of an alternative political and social order, offered with the intention and the hope of transforming present power structures and the ideas and values that support them.

Mannheim identified and thoughtfully analyzed four forms of "utopian mentality" in modern history:

1. The millennial "Chiliasm" of the Anabaptists in the Protestant Reformation, generating a "spiritualization of politics" from the most oppressed strata of society. What is startling in Mannheim's interpretation of the Anabaptists is that this intensely "spiritual" and "utopian" Christian movement marked the real beginning of "politics in the modern sense of the term . . ., if we here understand by politics a more or less conscious participation of all strata of society in the achievement of some mundane purpose, as contrasted with

a fatalistic acceptance of events as they are, or of control from 'above.' "[10] (Very interesting: politics begins with spirituality!)

2. The liberal humanitarianism of the Enlightenment, with its appeals to reason, the free will, the progress of science, republican institutions, and the vision of an indeterminate and unconditioned future.[11]

3. The conservative philosophy that developed a "counter-utopia" to the liberal evolutions and revolutions of the Enlightenment, viewing them as "vaporous and lacking in concreteness."[12]

4. The socialist-communist utopia that envisioned a new egalitarian order upon the breakdown of capitalist culture and institutions.[13] Here Mannheim observed that the Marxists and Leninists "unmasked all [their] adversaries' utopias as ideologies," but "never raised the problem of determinateness about [their] own position."[14]

Mannheim thus helps us to unmask the pretensions of the unmaskers, not only among Marxists and Leninists but also among Christian antagonists. The plain fact is that both his terms, *ideology* and *utopia,* all too often are made to serve as epithets or cusswords in political or religious combat. Like this: "You are an ideologue, obviously tainted by crass self-interest—or by heedless fanaticism." Or: "You are a utopian, a victim of your own harebrained fantasies." But: "I am a realist, with an objective, disinterested, and responsible approach to all things."

Claims to be a "realist," especially a "Christian realist," have for a half century been invoked against other Christians in theological and political controversies, along with the reproach that those others were mere "ideologues" or "utopians." Such polemics have cheapened discourse and have almost irretrievably discredited both ideology and utopia. It is a prime purpose of this book to redeem both words—*ideology* and *utopia*—and accord them imperative status among Christians, which is to say: Christian discipleship should impel us to become intentional ideologues and utopians, persons equipped with clarity of political beliefs and with visions of a transformed world.

Karl Mannheim's discussion of utopia lugubriously but eloquently concluded by imagining

a world in which there is never anything new, in which all is finished and each moment a repetition of the past, . . . in which thought will be utterly devoid of all ideological and utopian elements. But the complete elimination of reality-transcending elements from our world would lead us to a

16

"matter-of-factness" which ultimately would mean the decay of the human will. . . . The disappearance of utopia brings about a static state of affairs in which man himself becomes no more than a thing. We would be faced with the greatest paradox imaginable, namely, that man, who has achieved the highest degree of rational mastery of existence, left without any ideals, becomes a mere creature of impulses. Thus, after a long tortuous, but heroic development, just at the highest stage of awareness, when history is ceasing to be blind fate, and is becoming more and more man's own creation, with the relinquishment of utopias, man would lose his will to shape history and therewith his ability to understand it.[15]

Clearly implied in such a scenario is the conviction that both ideology and utopia are absolutely essential to making human life human—to safeguarding the freedom and creativity, the moral and spiritual vitality of persons and communities.

Forty years after Mannheim's apprehension over the possible "relinquishment of utopias," a powerful appeal for the "resurrection of utopias" came from a new band of liberation theologians. Rubem Alves, professor at the University of São Paulo, Brazil, declared: "The end of utopias is the end of ethical thought." In his *Theology of Human Hope,* Alves insisted that the renewal of utopian thinking is the basis for the renewal of Christian ethics itself. The essential task of Christian ethics is the liberation of the human imagination so that it can envision new utopias in contrast with all contemporary social systems. Without such utopian imagination, Christian ethics is reduced to piecemeal problem solving within the constraints of present systems. Alves's apparent familiarity with Mannheim is suggested in his invocation of two phrases from that last passage of Mannheim: Alves is convinced that when Christians no longer imagine utopias, they lose the "will to shape history" and thereby become "no more than a thing."[16]

A year later, in 1971, Gustavo Gutiérrez, a Peruvian priest, published his *Teología de la liberación* (the English translation, *A Theology of Liberation,* was published in 1973), which quickly established itself as the most influential text for and from liberation theologians. Close to the heart of Gutiérrez's theology is the positive role of utopia as a plan, grounded in historical reality, for "a qualitatively different society"—a plan that would "express the aspiration to establish new social relations" among people:

The historical plan, the utopia of liberation as the creation of a new social consciousness and as a social appropriation not only of the means of production, but also of the political process, and, definitively, of freedom, is the proper arena for the cultural revolution. . . . If utopia humanizes economic, social, and political liberation, this humanness—in the light of the Gospel—reveals God. . . . The Gospel does not provide a utopia for us; this is a human work.[17]

This imperative of utopias, of visions of alternative political and social systems, is not the exclusive claim of liberation theologians. It is the imperative of any Christian position that dares to hope that this society, or this world, does not have to be what it is now; that the poverty, tyranny, brutality, and rapacity of existing societies can and must be overcome. Such visions are the familiar treasures of the prophetic tradition in scripture: in Isaiah and Jeremiah, in the Gospels' promise of the coming reign of God, and in Revelation's hymn to that salvation in which long-suffering peoples "will hunger no more, and thirst no more; . . . and God will wipe away every tear from their eyes" (Rev. 7:16–17). Whether the churches can recover such treasures is really the great challenge of this ideological moment.

3

THE DENIAL
OF IDEOLOGY IN AMERICA

Ideology, which once was a road to action, has come to be a dead end.
—Daniel Bell, quoted in Waxman, ed.,
The End of Ideology Debate

The end-of-ideology is a slogan of complacency, circulating among the prematurely middle-aged . . . in the rich Western societies. . . . Second, the end-of-ideology is of course itself an ideology. . . . The end-of-ideology is on the way out because it stands for the refusal to work out an explicit political philosophy.
—C. Wright Mills, in Waxman, ed.,
The End of Ideology Debate

One of the main marks of American "exceptionalism"—that deeply felt confidence that, in the providence of God, this nation is qualitatively different from all others—has been the widely held belief that ideologies belong only to the Old World and not the New.

The resurgence of doctrinaire conservatism and neoconservatism since the 1970s must be understood, paradoxically, as an alternative expression of that same exceptionalism—but also as an exploitation of the seeming ideological vacuum after the political chaos of the 1960s. A time of ideological intensity has displaced the bipartisan pragmatism that dominated the period from the 1950s to the mid-1970s, which, in turn, had followed an earlier time of ideological intensity in the 1930s and 1940s. Nevertheless, the belief that the United States is a uniquely non-ideological society (itself a fervent ideological affirmation!) has persisted and has been expressed in several differing interpretations.

One variation holds that ours is an open-class society, unlike the historic European caste-and-class societies stemming from feudalism, monarchy, aristocracy, peasant revolution, and proletarian consciousness. Ideologies such as socialism, syndicalism, anarchism, communism, and fascism may be understood as products of such severe social stratification. The fact that none of these ideologies has succeeded in attracting a significant fraction of the American body politic is taken as proof of the social mobility of this "opportunity society." That proof is claimed in even more principled form when Americans declare that ideology and democracy are incompatible—it being assumed that ideology is to be re-garded pejoratively as authoritarian, intolerant, and the source of most of this century's horrors: world wars, Nazism, the Holocaust, Stalinism.

The dominant shape and style of American domestic politics through-out most of our history may seem to confirm this presumed lack of ide-ology. Our political parties have customarily functioned as loose aggre-gates of economic and sectional interests, not as unified bands of true believers divided along fundamental lines of political philosophy. Party discipline, whether in Congress or electoral politics, has been a weak and sometime thing. Interparty competition has normally been a struggle to occupy the platitudinous political center rather than the left or the right. (That the nature of political competition has changed dramatically since 1980 is a recurring theme in later chapters.) The watchwords of most po-litical veterans have traditionally tended to be *compromise, consensus, pragmatism,* and *incrementalism.*

These features of "the great game of politics" (to recall the title of a 1923 classic by Frank R. Kent, a shrewd participant-observer of the game) have been widely commended by legions of academics—political scientists, historians, economists, sociologists—many of whom have had their own professional aversions to ideology. The late Harold Lasswell, political scientist at Yale University, defined politics in clinically amoral and nonideological terms as "who gets what, when, and how" and again as "the study of influence and the influential."[1] In the 1950s and 1960s, prominent social scientists hailed "the end of ideology"—a slogan echoed in the highest ranks of U.S. government.

These widespread denials of the reality and/or the morality of ideology in America, whether by practitioners or scholars of our political system or by the general public, have been blessed by churches and theologians. The disavowal of ideology in the name of theological transcendence or for the sake of avoiding controversy and partisanship within the churches has reinforced the nation's self-image of moral exceptionalism. But it has also severely inhibited the ability of Christians to think and discuss ba-sic, principled issues of political economy, the common good, and peace-making.

A generation ago, in one of his many deeply thoughtful and ethically cogent books, the late Michael Harrington exposed these pretenses as amounting to an "anti-ideological ideology." In good humor, Harrington wrote:

> All of the politicians and most of the professors hold that this country is [a] blessedly unideological land where elections are naturally won at the Cen-ter rather than on the Right or Left. The utopianism of this no-nonsense creed is *not* so obvious since it is either shamefaced or unconscious. It is

found in the assumption that the world has been so benevolently created that the solutions to problems of revolutionary technological, economic and social change are invariably to be discovered in the middle of the road. Not since Adam Smith's invisible hand was thought to vector a myriad of private greeds into a common good has there been such a touching faith in secular providence.[2]

Harrington's ironic label for this "anti-ideological ideology" was "utopian pragmatism." At a time of rapid, systemic change, he insisted that the "real ideologues" were those "utopian pragmatists who believe that the society can bumble its way through a revolution." Such politicians and academics, he wrote, were "fanatics of moderation."[3]

Problems with Pragmatism

Pragmatism is undoubtedly a virtue among political virtues and a distinctly American contribution to philosophy and politics. In principle, pragmatism represents the wisdom of openness to experience, which is vitally important in social and international understanding. But pragmatism in practice, unguided by a significant social or political philosophy, may be defective at this very frontier of openness. It may work on small problems one-by-one without seeing the larger whole of policy and of history within which such piecemeal efforts at problem solving may be self-defeating. It suffers typically from an addiction to the structural status quo in society—even when the status is no longer quo!—while pretending that some problems can be solved once-for-all which may not really be soluble. Pragmatism chronically postpones for too long the necessity of acting at all for the sake of social justice; when it does act, it too often raises false hopes about what can then be quickly accomplished. In the American political style, both at home and abroad, pragmatism leads to an endless procession of crash programs (or wars on poverty, drugs, etc.) too long delayed. At a New York conference, the British economist Barbara Ward assessed U.S. development policies in the Third World, rather colorfully characterizing such a style as follows: "A crash program is like a man having an affair with nine women simultaneously, hoping to produce an offspring in one month." Pragmatism with its crash programs and Protestantism with its crusades for good moral causes are no doubt the closest of kin deep down in our national character. Both tend to provide escapes from systemic analysis and ideological direction. And at its worst, pragmatism, in its pretentious denial of ideological bias and its disdain for "ideologues," can be among the most insufferable of all ideologies.

The cool, liberal pragmatism that seemed in the ascendancy in the early 1960s became preoccupied with the "fine-tuning" of the economy, with technical adjustments, with incrementalism and piecemeal policies, with managing the equilibrium among interest groups and the bureaucratic programs that served them. In May 1962, at the White House Economic Conference, President John Kennedy announced that "most of the problems . . . are technical problems, are administrative problems [which] do not lend themselves to the great sort of 'passionate movements' which have stirred this country so often in the past." The following month, in an address at Yale University, Kennedy said:

> The central domestic problems of our time . . . do not relate to basic clashes of philosophy and ideology, but to ways and means . . . [to] sophisticated solutions to complex and obstinate problems. . . . Political labels and ideological approaches are irrelevant to the solutions. . . . Technical answers—not political answers—must be provided.[4]

These declarations of anti-ideological, technocratic pragmatism (astonishingly in retrospect) were made on the eve of the climactic civil rights revolution, the belated discovery of mass poverty, the burning of cities, and the war that destroyed the moral consensus on foreign policy, created the generation gap, spawned the New Left, unleashed severe inflation, and shattered millions of citizens' confidence in almost all basic institutions.

The cool pragmatism of New Frontier politicians was mentored and reinforced by hosts of ascendant academics in 1960 and for some years thereafter. The intellectual backdrop of liberal pragmatism in government was the domination of the social sciences by positivism—the assumption of a value-free, nonideological, behavioral and quantitative approach to society, economy, and politics.

The Beginning of "The End of Ideology"

The intellectual and historical judgment that Western societies, preeminently the United States, had arrived at "the end of ideology" was a main theme of an extraordinary international conference in Milan in September 1955. One hundred fifty scholars, politicians, and journalists convened by the Congress for Cultural Freedom spent a week discussing "The Future of Freedom." Among the American scholars present were three prominent sociologists, all of whom would soon become widely identified as exponents of "the end of ideology" thesis: Edward Shils, Seymour Martin Lipset, and Daniel Bell. (A dozen years after the Milan Conference, it was disclosed that the U.S. government had a distinctly anticommunist ideological investment in the Congress for Cultural Freedom through CIA funding laundered by "American foundations.")[5]

In his impassioned personal account of the "Future of Freedom" conference, titled "The End of Ideology?" Edward Shils wrote:

> The Milan Conference showed us how much we still have to do. For decades the proponents of freedom have been struggling against National Socialism, Fascism, and Bolshevism, on the battlefield, in the legislative chamber, and in the study. . . . We no longer feel the need for a comprehensive explicit system of beliefs. . . . There are great tasks to be undertaken amidst the ruin of the ideologies. We must reconstruct our beliefs without yielding to the temptation to construct new ideologies, as rigid, as eager for consistency and for universal observance as those which have been now transcended.[6]

Shils went on to plead for the rediscovery of "the permanently valid elements in our historical ideals."[7]

Those passages reveal the semantic confusion and apparent contradictions in the preachings of the "end of ideology" advocates. The assumed definition of ideology is wholly negative and aimed at political phenomena in other countries, while we Americans are to recover "historical ideals" and "reconstruct our beliefs"—although "ideals" and "beliefs" are not the same as an ideology, and we need not be explicit, or comprehensive, or consistent in formulating those beliefs.

Seymour Martin Lipset posed the same issues, under the very same title, "The End of Ideology?" in the last chapter of his 1960 work, *Political Man*. Lipset declared that the traditional issues dividing left from right had become insignificant by the 1950s. Why? Because

> the fundamental political problems of the industrial revolution have been solved: the workers have achieved industrial and political citizenship; the conservatives have accepted the welfare state; and the democratic left has recognized that an increase in over-all state power carries with it more dangers to freedom than solutions for economic problems. This very triumph of the democratic social revolution in the West ends domestic politics for those intellectuals who must have ideologies or utopias to motivate them to political action.[8]

In the 1990s, it is obvious that these almost eschatological judgments have long since become nullified, not least in view of the virtual repudiation of the welfare state by the dominant leadership of the Republican Party.

The third of these eminent sociologists, Daniel Bell, attracted the most attention to the "end of ideology" thesis by the pronunciamiento title of his 1960 book, *The End of Ideology*. Bell, who had been a left-wing anti-Stalinist socialist in the 1930s, characterized the two decades 1930–1950 as having "an intensity peculiar in written history," given the Depression, class struggles, rise of fascism, World War II, concentration camps, and death chambers.[9] But in America, as in the West generally, a political consensus had been achieved on "acceptance of a Welfare State; the desirability of decentralized power; a system of mixed economy and of political pluralism."[10] With that achievement, ideology, "which once was a road to action, has come to a dead end."[11]

Bell grandly regarded ideology historically as the modern successor to religion, marked by the same appeals to faith, passion, and irrationality. But now the day of ideology, too, was done because of the technical sophistication of social science and the maturity of the politics of consensus. Or so thought Daniel Bell in 1960.

A strong undercurrent in this analysis was the confession that *socialism* had come to a dead end and that Daniel Bell and numerous other onetime-socialist ideologues had at last come to terms with Franklin Roosevelt's New Deal, the welfare state, and the unprecedented prosperity of the United States in the postwar years. In still later years, that prosperity could more soberly be understood as something besides the triumph of sound domestic economic policies: it owed much to the enormous stimulus of wartime production and the unchallenged postwar economic supremacy of a nation whose productive institutions had not been devastated by that war.

Now we must take account of an extraordinary fact about Messrs. Shils, Lipset, Bell, and others of the "end of ideology" sect. They who did so much to clear the stage of legitimate ideological options in the 1960s came back on stage themselves in the 1970s as aggressive neoconservative ideologues. That fact exposes their contradictions—or perhaps their mind changes. But in another sense it highlights a certain consistency, for after all, the end of ideology presumption led to an apology for things as they are (or were). Notwithstanding the prior Marxist credentials of many of them, or their continuing liberal rhetoric, they had become rather conservative years before they would be called neoconservative. And as neoconservatives clustered around the American Enterprise Institute, they became more and more identified with the promotion of business interests.

Christians of more progressive views thus confront two seemingly opposite conservative challenges: the anti-ideological strictures from self-styled pragmatists and the aggressive ideological assaults from neoconservative sectarians and the Religious Right. And many of the selfsame adversaries have personified both challenges, opposite though they may be, but at different moments in their careers.

For Christians seeking a principled political ethic, the end of ideology myth—and it is a myth!—implies precisely the opposite: the separation of ethics from politics at their very foundations. The disavowal of ideology in favor of intellectual positivism and political pragmatism disconnects the moral purposes of government from the concrete responsibilities of political action. *To annul ideology is to demoralize politics.*

Philosophical Repudiations

In addition to the positivism and pragmatism of some social scientists, the moral commitments of some political philosophers repelled by the "isms" of the 1930s and 1940s have led to categorical condemnations of all ideologies. Hannah Arendt's 1973 work, *The Origins of Totalitarianism,* repudiated the "totalitarian elements that are peculiar to all ideological thinking." Among those elements, she wrote, are the insistence on a "truth" not perceptible by outsiders and the pretense "to know the mysteries of the whole historical process—the secrets of the past, the intricacies of the present, the uncertainties of the future." Ideologies demand an absolutist logic that proceeds deductively from a basic premise "with a consistency that exists nowhere in the realm of reality." In short, according to Arendt, ideologies are inherently antidemocratic and inevitably totalitarian.[12] Her depiction of ideologies certainly fits fascism and the more authoritarian models of Marxism-Leninism. But it raises again the problem of definition of ideology, which she draws extremely narrowly and negatively.

Arendt's categorical negative is shared by Catholic University political philosopher David Walsh, whose 1990 book, *After Ideology,* demanded "the exposure of the moral bankruptcy of all ideological forms of thought. No shred of an excuse must be left to disguise their responsibility for the enormity of evil they have wrought within our time."[13] Walsh rebuked not only "the failure to resist the military advances of totalitarianism, whether fascist, national socialist, or Communist, but also the deeper historical responsibility of liberalism that spawned the revolutionary movements."[14] For Walsh—as for legions of politicians and theologians and self-styled evangelicals—liberalism (whatever that is) is the scapegoat for most of the horrors of modern history. Imprecision in the definition of liberalism is one of the most befogging factors in academic, political, and religious discourse. For Walsh, moreover, the imprecise notion of ideology itself, along with its presumed wickedness, tends to provide an escape from some of the central issues in political philosophy. Curiously, however, he concludes by appealing to such ideas as "the spiritual foundation of liberal democracy," recognition of the family as "the preferred interpersonal foundation of society," the "autonomy" of education, and the "crucial role played by all forms of voluntary associations"—as if such notions were nonideological. It would seem that the author of *After Ideology* is, after all—as we all are—an ideological creature.

What if, instead of regarding democracy and ideology as antithetical (as Arendt and Walsh do), we prefer to view democracy itself as an ideology, albeit an open, dynamic, and flexible ideology? Doesn't a mature democratic faith require a set of beliefs and symbols that serve to interpret social reality and to motivate political action? Some of the elements of democracy as an ideology, in the form of "democratic humanism," are suggested in chapter 9.

Theological Disavowals

If some politicians, social scientists, and philosophers can find reasons for denying the legitimacy of ideology, it is hardly surprising to discover that some theologians and some churches can do and have done the same. From the 1930s to the 1960s, the messages of the world ecumenical movement consistently referred to ideologies in only pejorative terms. Of course, those messages were mindful of the same horrors unleashed by the totalitarianisms of those years that outraged political leaders, sociologists, and philosophers. The founding Amsterdam Assembly of the World Council of Churches (WCC) in 1948, an event long delayed by the world's ghastliest war and set in the opening rounds of the Cold War, called on the churches "to reject the ideologies of both communism and laissez-faire capitalism," without presuming to commend an alternative model.[15] At its inauguration, the World Council's theological and political perspectives had clearly been shaped by the continental and ecclesial struggles of Europe.

It was not until 1966, at the Geneva World Conference on Church and Society, that world ecumenism managed to articulate a less pejorative, actually a rather positive, conception of ideology. The WCC had recently focused on "rapid social change," especially in the decolonized Third World, and in 1961 had welcomed into membership churches from the Soviet Union. A main theme of the Geneva Conference was the variety of revolutions—national, social, technical—occurring at that time, along with the upsurge of New Left politics in the United States and the West, especially provoked by the war in Indochina and the intense hostility between the United States and the People's Republic of China. At Geneva, conferees defined ideology as "the theoretical and analytical structure of thought which undergirds successful action to realize revolutionary change in society or to undergird and justify its status quo."[16] The positive half of that definition was an anticipation of the ideological and utopian perspectives of the liberation theologians that would be announced several years later.

The most influential American theologian from the 1930s to the 1960s was Reinhold Niebuhr, a formidable figure in global ecumenism as well as in American political thought. A quasi-Marxist in the 1930s and a founder of the Fellowship of Socialist Christians in 1935, Niebuhr gradually moved toward a nonideological pragmatism. He resigned his Socialist Party membership in 1940. In 1953, he sharply criticized socialism and declared that "the discrediting of the Marxist dogma in all of its varieties and not merely in its most noxious form, should convince us . . . to be grateful for a democratic society which manages to extract a measure of truth from the contest of contrasting errors."[17] In truth, Niebuhr was never, at any stage, a systematic political philosopher or theologian.

Niebuhr's disavowal of ideology, his growing faith in democracy, and his embrace of pragmatism—all of which he could and did rationalize theologically—made him a de facto confederate of the "end of ideology" circle in the 1950s and 1960s. His earlier economic radicalism yielded to the judgment shared by Shils, Lipset, and Bell that the American economy had achieved a "proximate justice" and had solved its most serious problems. After Niebuhr's death in 1971, some rising neoconservatives would claim to be his political and ethical heirs—to the consternation of his more progressive followers.

A more consistent theme in Niebuhr's works, whether from a socialist or a pragmatist base, or from a theological appeal to "the transcendent God of Hebrew and Christian faith," was his repudiation of utopianism. In fact, almost all of his adversaries of whatever persuasion were likely to be put down as "utopian" in the name of "Christian Realism." Marxists, democratic socialists, capitalists, liberals, pacifists all were caught up in their "illusions." In *An Interpretation of Christian Ethics* (1935), Niebuhr wrote: "Utopianism must inevitably lead to disillusionment. . . . It has no means of discovering that its visions and dreams are relative to partial interests and temporary perspectives and that even the universal element in them will lose its universality and unqualifiedness when it is made concrete in history."[18]

This more accommodating, professedly nonideological and antiutopian Niebuhr and legions who followed him would become, in the 1960s and after, the foil for many liberation theologians, democratic socialists, and assorted liberals who sought to reconstruct ideologies and resurrect utopias. However, no post-Niebuhrian religious thinker has begun to match Niebuhr's own influence or to offer a comprehensive and compelling new political philosophy.

In 1971, the year of Reinhold Niebuhr's death, a young seminary student in suburban Chicago emerged as an evangelical prophet on issues of war and racism, launching a magazine and a community that would move to Washington and be known as Sojourners. Jim Wallis added poverty, sexism, and gang warfare to his evangelical agenda. In 1994, he published a 250-page midcareer manifesto and memoir, *The Soul of Politics*—an appeal for a "vision of transformation."

Wallis's notion of transformation, however, is relentlessly anti-ideology. To be "spiritual" and "prophetic," according to Wallis, is to seek the end of ideology. In particular, he reproaches both the Left and the Right, liberalism and conservatism: liberalism for its alleged captivity to "impersonal bureaucracies that are more concerned with control than caring"; conservatism for its "lack of a strong ethic of social responsibility."[19]

But Wallis's repudiation of ideology is even more thoroughgoing. The moral issues now at stake in American society must not be "manipulated and twisted" for "ideological purposes."[20]

> There are periods in history when social crisis threatens to unravel society. But such times are often also eras of transition, invitation, and opportunity. . . . At these historical junctures, ideological analysis and solutions are inadequate. . . . Rather, a new spirituality is required, a spirituality rooted in old traditions but radically applied to our present circumstances.[21]

Such a "spirituality" disdains any search for "new macroeconomic systems to replace the ideological dinosaurs that have failed us."[22] Or again: "This movement of prophetic conscience is political without being ideological."[23]

There is an antigovernmental animus in Wallis's writings that tends to resonate with all those who, like Ronald Reagan, relish declaring that you have to get away from Washington (especially to the Sunbelt and the Midwest) to meet "real people" and understand "real problems." However, there is a real-world perspective Wallis claims "from waking up in one of the poorest and most violent neighborhoods of Washington, D.C." where the Sojourners community is located. Striking a similar populist note, Wallis declares that "the reality of this country cannot be understood from inside the offices of Washington lobbyists, media pundits, and politicians who inhabit the corridors of power."[24] (Can we therefore assume that there is more wisdom among the statehouse lobbyists of the Cotton Belt, or the newspaper chains of the Corn Belt, or the courthouse gangs of California?)

Jim Wallis's combination of evangelical theology and social passion has unquestionably helped recruit many conservative Christians to projects of social service and action. His courageous activism, such as his reconciling intervention in gang violence, has won him special respect around the nation and the world. However, his seemingly centrist scolding of both Left and Right, his stereotypical portraits of "liberals" and "bureaucrats," his contempt for political institutions, and his repudiation of ideology without articulating an alternative political philosophy have made his style of witness problematical for conceiving the actual "visions of transformation" he professes. Lacking such an ideology or political philosophy and disdaining the effort to imagine "new macroeconomic systems," Wallis risks settling for the piecemeal pragmatism of particular projects, however "spiritual" or "prophetic" their motivation.

Ideology, if constructively and comprehensively imagined, at least confronts the complex realities of social and political systems and their human consequences—and thereby dares to offer well-wrought visions for overcoming systemic injustice.

4

THE REALITY
OF IDEOLOGY IN AMERICA

We hold these Truths to be self-evident, that all Men are created equal, that they are endowed by their Creator with certain unalienable Rights, that among these are Life, Liberty, and the Pursuit of Happiness—That to secure these Rights, Governments are instituted among Men, deriving their just Powers from the Consent of the Governed.
                    —*The Declaration of Independence* (1776)

The dogmas of the quiet past, are inadequate to the stormy present. The occasion is piled high with difficulty, and we must rise with the occasion. As our case is new, so we must think anew, and act anew. We must disenthrall ourselves. . . . *We* cannot escape history. . . . We shall nobly save, or meanly lose, the last best, hope of earth. . . . The way is plain, peaceful, generous, just—a way which, if followed, the world will forever applaud, and God must forever bless.
                                        —Abraham Lincoln

The business of America is business.
            —Calvin Coolidge

The disavowal of ideology by theology seems particularly bizarre in a nation whose political culture, from its very beginnings, has been suffused with religious ideas and symbols. Most Americans have believed that theirs is a "redeemer nation"[1] whose history and destiny have been uniquely shaped by God's providence: its "virgin birth" on an "empty" continent; founding saints (Washington, Jefferson, Madison, and others); canonical texts (Declaration of Independence, Constitution, Gettysburg Address); sanctuary for immigrants; model of democracy and God-given human rights; benevolence to the world's suffering peoples; prosperity as the reward for national virtue, free enterprise, and "American know-how"; victory in world wars and the Cold War as divine vindication of the mission of America to liberate the world.

A variety of terms has been concocted to identify such religious themes in the nation's public rhetoric. In 1969, sociologist Robert Bellah reintroduced Rousseau's notion of a "civil religion" and characterized its American form as "not the worship of the American nation but an understanding of the American experience in the light of ultimate and universal reality." American civil religion, according to Bellah, is neither sec-

30

tarian nor specifically Christian, yet it is specifically American and has served as "a genuine vehicle of national religious self-understanding." Although he acknowledges its recurrent abuse as "a cloak for petty interests and ugly passions," he nonetheless maintains that it is "a heritage of moral and religious experience from which we still have much to learn as we formulate the decisions that lie ahead."

> Behind the civil religion at every point lie Biblical archetypes: Exodus, Chosen People, Promised Land, New Jerusalem, Sacrificial Death and Rebirth.
> . . . It has its own prophets and its own martyrs, its own sacred events and sacred places, its own solemn rituals and symbols. It is concerned that America be a society as perfectly in accord with the will of God as men can make it, and a light to all nations.[2]

Church historian Martin Marty prefers the concept of "public theology" to denote "an effort to interpret the life of a people in the light of a transcendent reference." Marty insists that a public theology is not the same as the civil religion, which, he says, tends to obscure the pluralism of the American experience. Nevertheless, a public theology "focuses on 'ordering faith,' which helps constitute civil, social, and political life from a theological point of view."[3] As an exemplar, Martin Luther King, Jr. is cited by Marty for his God-centered vision that drew on the Declaration of Independence, the Constitution, and the rhetoric of Abraham Lincoln.

The Paradoxes of American Ideology

Such prominent religious themes among the nation's political ideas may not be coherently related to those ideas, much less control or dominate them. In a recent work mournfully titled *The Poverty of American Politics,* political scientist H. Mark Roelofs distinguishes between the functions of *mythology* and *ideology* in the political system. According to Roelofs, the function of mythology is to legitimize the nation and its government. In the United States, religious ideas, especially from the Protestant heritage, define the basic myths of legitimacy. Mythology thus becomes what Marty had called a "public theology." On the other hand, the function of ideology is to rationalize the actual structure and workings of the political system. In the United States, writes Roelofs, the ideology is secular and bourgeois.

Roelofs thus sees a bifurcation between American myths and American ideology—"a double system of principles, institutions, and processes that are in near constant contradiction with each other." At its core, the contradiction is between the nation's religious mythology and its constitutional identity as a secular state. "The central paradox of American politics is that it is driven to be both an egalitarian, community-loving social democracy seeking broad goals of social justice, and, at the same time, a freedom-loving, privatistic, interest-seeking liberal democracy with powerfully sustained elitist tendencies."[4] This contrast between two different versions of the meaning of democracy—the religious imperative of social justice for the individual and the secular promise of liberal license for the individual—is embodied in what Roelofs calls "the Protestant/Bourgeois Complex." In that complex of contradiction and paradox,

> the Protestant and Bourgeois elements of American individualism are, simultaneously, radically united in their celebration of the radical autonomy of the individual, and, as radically, divided by the absolute irreconcilability of the demands they respectively place on the individual. In consequence, American individualism, the rock on which all else in the American political system is built, is itself, at core, radically schizophrenic.[5]

The systemic consequences of this "Protestant/Bourgeois Complex" are deep-seated institutional fissures, the crippling of government, and ultimately the "poverty of American politics." In particular, this means official double-talk, irrational budgeting, uncontrollable bureaucracies, spells of military adventurism and foreign policy quagmires, increasingly fatuous campaigns and elections, and mass frustration with government and politics.

We need not accept Roelofs' distinction between mythology and ideology, nor all his empirical judgments about the performance of the political system, in order to perceive the painful truths in his account of the radical schizophrenia between Protestant heritage and secular realities. (Myths, after all, can be counted among the elements of an ideology and not as ideas apart from it.)

Paradox, schizophrenic individualism, moral dualism are all terms with a long history as attempts to define the ideological faults in American politics. In the 1830s, Alexis de Tocqueville's *Democracy in America* discerned a peculiar paradox in the American character: Americans were simultaneously a people of intense spiritualism and unrestrained materialism. "Although the desire of acquiring the good things of this world is the prevailing passion of the American people, certain momentary outbreaks occur when their souls seem suddenly to burst the bonds of matter by which they are restrained and to soar impetuously toward heaven."[6] Such a characteristic vividly presaged Roelofs' notion of the "Protestant/Bourgeois Complex," although he does not acknowledge Tocqueville as a source for it.

In *Pious and Secular America* Reinhold Niebuhr, always much attracted to notions of paradox and irony, similarly portrayed modern Americans as

> at once the most religious and the most secular of Western nations. . . . We are "religious" in the sense that religious communities enjoy the devotion

and engage the active loyalty of more laymen than in any nation in the Western world. We are "secular" in the sense that we pursue the immediate goals of life, without asking too many ultimate questions about the meaning of life and without being too disrupted by the tragedies and antinomies of life.[7]

Any ideology or public theology that fails to deal with this paradoxical spiritual/materialistic, religious/secular, moralistic/pragmatic complex is bound to be captive to the interests of the rich and insensitive to the suffering of the poor.

The imperative of ideological reconstruction derives especially from this: that the United States of America is the richest country in the world, with the richest churches in the world, at a time when the great gulf between the rich and the poor, in both America and the world-at-large, continues to expand catastrophically. These are human flesh-and-blood facts that neither the present rhetoric of American politics nor the present priorities of American government seem prepared to recognize. Indeed, it is difficult to demonstrate that the rhetoric and priorities of American churches in the 1990s have been much more cognizant of these facts.

The moral dualism of American nationhood has long been projected onto other nations. In 1845, on the eve of the expansionist Mexican War (which cost Mexico the loss of California, Nevada, Utah, Colorado, Arizona, New Mexico, Wyoming, and all claims to Texas north of the Rio Grande), President James Polk delivered an inaugural address that was remarkably schizophrenic in its moral claims:

> Foreign powers do not seem to appreciate the true character of our Government. Our union is a confederation of independent states, whose policy is peace with each other and all the world. To enlarge its limits is to extend the dominions of peace over additional territories and increasing millions. The world has nothing to fear from military ambition in our government.[8]

That is an imperial projection of national interest that asks the world to believe in the *dis*-interested benevolence of America's peaceful intentions. Mexican memory has a keener sense of that moral dualism than does U.S. memory.

Even this emphasis on the paradoxical and contradictory elements in American ideology amounts to an oversimplification, for there are many and diverse beliefs widely shared among Americans who do not necessarily worry about the coherence of such beliefs. Samuel Huntington writes: "The basic ideas of the American Creed—equality, liberty, individualism, constitutionalism, democracy—clearly do not constitute a systematic ideology, and they do not necessarily have any logical consistency."[9]

The Ideological Mainstream

Nevertheless, there is a conspicuous ideological stream through American history that has picked up new and diverse currents along the way, every half century or so, sweeping most Americans along with it. It is a powerful stream of great moral vitality and great ethical ambiguity.

At the source of this ideological mainstream is a Puritan Ethos, which mixed a messianic conceit of a chosen people—a covenantal New Israel under the providence of God—with a heavy moralism that made original sin a basic doctrine of both government and economics, and activism a definition of lifestyle. Perry Miller has provided a definitive historical perspective on this prime source of American "exceptionalism":

> The Puritan state was seen by Puritans as the incarnation of their collective will; it was driven by an energy they had acquired in their conversion, it was the embodied image of their power, of their resolution, of their idea. . . . New England political theory made the state almost a kind of second incarnation, a Messiah fathered by God and born of the people. Mortal men, being visited by God in the Covenant of Grace, conceive a will to moral obedience; when they covenant among themselves, when they combine their several regenerate wills into one all-inclusive will, the state becomes another savior, the child of God and man, leading men to righteousness and preparing them for the final reckoning.[10]

The individualistic Protestant ethic, too often attributed to the Puritans, actually owed more to the exiles from, and the opponents of, the Puritans. After all, the Puritans maintained a heavy covenantal emphasis on community and conformity. In contrast, the free churches, especially Baptists and Methodists, were "the true entrepreneurs of American religion." They provided early sanctions for what would become the rugged individualism of the frontier and the morality (or antimorality) of "the survival of the fittest."[11] So it was that not only the precepts of the Puritans but also the conflicts generated by the Puritans that decisively shaped the paradoxes of ideology at the sources of American nationhood.

An "agrarian fundamentalism" was nurtured in the early decades of American identity—a socioreligious orientation that would persist through all the generations of industrialization and urbanization and continue to shape majoritarian attitudes even when the farming population shrank to a single-digit minority. In fact, even the ascendant religious and political forces of the 1990s, in the postindustrial age of cyberspace, drew largely on the myth-loaded texts of agrarian fundamentalism in their assaults on "liberalism," the welfare state, and affirmative action. Richard Hofstadter's characterization of the differences between the village agriculture of Europe and the frontier agriculture of America helps us to understand the pristine sources of American individualism:

The predominance in American agriculture of the isolated farmstead standing in the midst of great acreage, the frequent movements, the absence of village life, deprived the farmer and his family of the advantages of community, lowered the chances of association and cooperation, and encouraged that rampant, suspicious, and almost suicidal individualism for which the American farmer was long noted and which organizations like the Grange tried to combat. The characteristic product of American rural society was not a yeoman or a villager, but a harassed little country businessman who worked very hard, moved all too often, gambled with his land, and made his way alone.[12]

These primal currents were joined by an Enlightenment Rationalism (itself generated largely by English Puritanism) that saw the new American covenant become a social contract based on natural rights, the exaltation of individual dignity, freedom, and equality, a minimal libertarian view of government, and an optimistic faith in reason and science.

The most precious American contribution to the common ideological treasury of the world was the foundational philosophy of human rights. Although that philosophy drew on English (especially Lockean) and other sources, its grounding in creation doctrine and its covenantal basis in American constitutionalism proved to be of enduring, exemplary, and immeasurable universal significance. Any contemporary reconstruction of American ideology would do well to celebrate that tradition and build upon it.

Thomas Jefferson became the icon of the nation's Enlightenment heritage and the premier American philosopher of democracy as freedom and equality. But Jefferson's ideological legacy proved to be highly ambiguous. What was seemingly coherent in the late eighteenth century would turn out to be contradictory in the nineteenth and twentieth centuries. A distinction between a "people ideology" (about human nature and society) and a "power ideology" (about the structure of government) helps to interpret this ambiguity. Jefferson's egalitarian people ideology proclaimed an optimistic view of human nature, its rational and moral potential, and the sanctity of individual rights. The people closest to his heart were the farmers and artisans of rural and small-town America. His power ideology, while it exalted majority rule, emphasized local autonomy, states' rights, and a weak and strictly limited federal government, lest it become a powerful tool of commercial, banking, and industrial interests.

In later generations, Jefferson's power ideology would be invoked to frustrate the legitimate heirs of his people ideology. States' rights would be proclaimed against civil rights. A laissez-faire dogma of narrowly limited government would permit rapacious commercial and industrial interests to go unregulated, then to be challenged by Jefferson's people ideology to bless the New Deal and the developing welfare state.

The egalitarianism of Jefferson and the Declaration of Independence was countered by the original Constitution's deference to the propertied and slaveholding aristocracies. Moreover, the Constitution implicitly offered a more somber Calvinist view of human nature, reflected in its structured suspicion of power—a government of separated and federally divided powers. In *Federalist Paper 51,* James Madison wrote:

> Ambition must be made to counteract ambition. . . . What is government itself but the greatest of all reflections on human nature? If men were angels, no government would be necessary. If angels were to govern men, neither external nor internal controls on government would be necessary.

For want of "better motives," the selfish, rival interests of sinful men, whether government officials or private citizens, must be deliberately structured in opposition to one another.[13]

The industrial, commercial, and financial interests that Jefferson had so vigorously opposed increasingly defined the political culture after 1800. A *Business Mystique* that could begin with the mercantilism championed by Alexander Hamilton (that is, a strong government to promote business interests) evolved toward its seeming opposite, *laissez-faire* (that is, a government too weak to regulate or control enterprise, but no less devoted to its promotion). The consistent fact is that America has been a business civilization since 1800, a fact celebrated by presidents and lamented by social critics. Historian Richard Hofstadter, in his 1964 Pulitzer Prize–winning book *Anti-Intellectualism in American Life,* judged that "business is the most powerful and pervasive interest in American life"—and that "business [is] in the vanguard of anti-intellectualism in our culture."[14]

In the early nineteenth century, American capitalism and egalitarian democracy developed a certain affinity that would endure through the Republican presidency of Abraham Lincoln. The concept of "The Common Man" that flourished in the era of Jacksonian Democracy (1825–1860) was allied to the ideas of equality, competition, individualism, and laissez-faire. Jefferson's power ideology still seemed feasible to many libertarian democrats in the pre–Civil War years and also served the interests of the rising business class. "The same forces in American life that had made Jacksonian equalitarianism possible and had given to the equalitarian theme in the agrarian romance its most compelling appeal had also unleashed in the nation an entrepreneurial zeal probably without precedent in history, a rage for business, for profits, for opportunity, for advancement."[15] Ralph Waldo Emerson and Henry David Thoreau, remembered most for their liberal preaching of self-reliant individualism, also preached the minimal government of laissez-faire.

In time, the relentless march of the Industrial Revolution through agrarian America, spearheaded by railroad monopolies, would intensify a class struggle that the individualistic egalitarian faith tried to deny. On the margins of this developing business civilization, however, a host of new social movements emerged: abolitionism, women's rights, prohibition, prison reform, labor organizations, utopian cooperative communities. All these, in turn, combined to inculcate reformism and voluntarism as fresh currents in the ideological stream, even if their particular causes were frustrated.

It was not until after the Civil War and the emerging hegemony of the probusiness Republican Party that laissez-faire became decisively transmuted from liberal egalitarianism into conservative dogma. That dogma was adorned with the dynamic new evolutionary doctrines of *Social Darwinism*—the deceitful paradox of aggressive corporatism in the name of individualism and the survival of the fittest, meaning moral contempt for poor people. The Protestant ethic had increasingly become bourgeois religiosity as Protestant churches became increasingly middle class, estranged from workers, and beholden to pillars of business and banking. The characteristic social role of many Protestant churches became, as Roelofs put it, that of "sentinels" for "the nation's Bourgeois, secular order."

> On the one hand, they lauded Bourgeois needs and endlessly praised and otherwise rewarded Bourgeois successes. Middle-class and upper-middle-class churches . . . became bastions of Bourgeois self-congratulation, compliments the Bourgeoisie generously returned with lavish material support for the churches and their various special projects. On the other hand, a soft Christianity of spiritualism and social fellowship served to hide the hard, rapacious character of America's operative political system and its business-oriented civilization. The poor were actively mystified. A flow of good works spilled like syrup over the nation's persistent and fundamental social ills. Americans were told—and largely came to believe—that they were truly and actively a Christian people.[16]

Thus did the Business Mystique become increasingly legitimized morally by its ostentatious philanthropies, such as Carnegie libraries and new theological seminaries funded by ascendant millionaires. The political significance of all this for the churches was further explicated by Roelofs: "Even as the hierarchies of government and business shamelessly used religion to legitimize themselves and their activities—and in return generously awarded the churches with tax exemptions and other subsidies—they fastened on the churches not only the doctrine of the separation of church and state" but its presumed religious implication: "that religion has nothing to do with politics because religion is a purely personal and spiritual business."[17] But the overriding interests were rationalized by the credo of business virtue and efficiency against government corruption and incompetence—a mask that served to obscure the multitudinous ways in which business corporations in the late 1800s were themselves prime corruptors of government at every level.

The everlasting myth of the Business Mystique continues to hold that business is good, while government is bad, and, more and more, that big business is good and big government is bad. The antipolitical, antigovernmental moralisms of so many middle-class Protestants, together with their privatized religiosity and their aversion to political controversies within their churches, continue to conscript them for service to the idols of the Business Mystique.

Progress and Pragmatism

The relentless flow of messianism, individualism, and evolutionism had by the late nineteenth century shaped a uniquely American Faith in Progress. That faith especially celebrated the American Dream of social mobility and prosperity, the sanctity of public education, and the infinite capacities of technology—as in "good old American know-how." But this optimistic faith also prompted, not surprisingly, a Progressive movement outraged by the abuses of predatory capitalism and its grip on government, and dedicated to purposeful intervention in the evolutionary development of the country. Reformism thus became popular, even the platform of much of the political establishment for a few years early in the twentieth century. The ideas of positive government, direct democracy (as in primary elections, the initiative, the referendum, and the recall), economic democracy, and environmental conservation swelled the ideological stream.

The Progressive movement had a very short life, yielding to the resurgence of Social Darwinism in the 1920s ("Back to Normalcy" was the triumphal theme of Warren G. Harding's ascent to the presidency in the election of 1920). But Social Darwinism, just as soon, had to yield to a new reformism in the face of the economic distress and political turbulence of the Depression of the 1930s. Liberal Pragmatism rose up with Franklin Delano Roosevelt and his New Deal. The business credo of laissez-faire was thrown on the defensive as never before. Government became activist and experimental across almost the entire agenda of economic life, welfare, environment, and energy. A "mixed economy" largely devoid of either traditional capitalist or socialist doctrine defined the new majority consensus. And a war that both defeated the Axis powers and destroyed the imperial hegemonies of the European Allies provided an unprecedented stimulus to the productivity and postwar prosperity of the American economy. That war left the United States, as the greatest of world powers, in a position to design the architecture of international organization, to dominate world currency and trade, to lift the American Dream to undreamed-of heights, to help massively in reconstructing the economies of both Allies and former enemies, and to threaten the annihilation of any new enemy. Thus American messianism seemed validated at last by incomparable wealth and power.

But long before World War II provided such a boon to American hegemony, the material facts of American history were conspiring to vindicate the pretensions of ideology. First of all, this nation acquired abundant land and vast resources on the North American continent that had nothing to do with capitalism or any other "ism"—nor with any fatuous notion that God's special providence had been withheld from other, presumably less virtuous and pious, peoples. Much of the land was simply stolen from other nations in the blood of conquest, especially from the great indigenous nations of Native Americans and from Mexico.

The productivity, prosperity, and global preeminence of the United States, then, may have other sources than economic ideology, or moral virtue, or divine providence. Ideology may not tell half the story, but it is a powerful political force commixing grace, greed, and fortune in the mythology of American nationhood.

This swift ride through the rapids of American political and economic heritage is intended only to suggest that ideology has been with us all the way. Very few if any of the currents that have joined the mainstream have really been lost along the way. American political beliefs and values today remain a mixture of the Puritan Ethos, Agrarian Fundamentalism, Enlightenment Rationalism, Business Mystique, Faith in Progress, and Liberal Pragmatism—all tending to focus on a highly individualistic mythology of the meaning of democracy. That there are positive virtues, as well as problematical distortions, in each of these currents is not to be doubted.

There is no escape from ideology in America: not into a science that pretends to be value-free, nor into a politics that claims to be strictly pragmatic and technical, nor into a theology that presumes to transcend all political or social or economic interests.

5

THE REGRESSIVE REVOLUTION I: ANTISTATISM

The supply-side approach was in fact so well known to the founders of the United States that it can claim to be the foundation of the American economic tradition.

—James Ring Adams, quoted in Blumenthal,
The Rise of the Counter-Establishment

Supply-side's birth coincided with the birth of Christ and Christianity.
—Jude Wanniski, quoted in Blumenthal,
The Rise of the Counter-Establishment

Through their making of a far-flung network [the conservatives] attempted to conquer political society. Their factories of ideology—think tanks, institutes, and journals—would win legitimacy for notions that would be translated into policy.

—Sidney Blumenthal,
The Rise of the Counter-Establishment

In the 1970s, an aggressive array of right-wing groups began to coalesce around a regressive ideological agenda. The rhetoric of that agenda ostentatiously exploited several traditional currents in the American ideological mainstream, notably the Puritan Ethos, Agrarian Fundamentalism, the Business Mystique—and individualism.

This Regressive Revolution, largely generated and funded by corporate and foundation largesse, brought disparate groups together in a political onslaught that would saturate the media, elect Ronald Reagan to the presidency, consolidate its control of the Republican Party, capture Congress, curb the welfare state, and assault public and higher education and the mainline churches.

Among the groups sharing in this onslaught were such longtime conservative pundits as William Buckley (editor of *National Review*); probusiness papers like *The Wall Street Journal;* nouveaux riches Sunbelt entrepreneurs; Bible Belt fundamentalists (like Jerry Falwell) recruited by secular political action committees; academic economists like Chicago monetarist Milton Friedman; and, most especially, a host of in-your-face "neoconservative" intellectuals among journalists, social scientists, and theologians.

The Varieties of Conservatism

If for shorthand reference this Regressive Revolution is called "conservative," that label can be seriously misleading if too broadly applied. It not only can obscure the diversity within the coalition; it can mistakenly associate with that coalition many persons and groups whose own conservatism has little in common with the coalition's agenda.

There is a conservatism grounded in humility of the nation before a sovereign God of justice, in equality of God-given human rights, in respect for the historic achievements and positive responsibilities of government for the general welfare, in preservation of culture and the arts against the outrages of tawdry commercial exploitation, and in conservation of nature and its life-supporting, life-enriching treasures for all future generations. Such a conservatism is neither right-wing nor left-wing, neither probusiness nor antibusiness, neither Republican nor Democrat. But it is a conservatism more trashed than celebrated by the main cohorts of the Regressive Revolution.

It would be grossly inaccurate and unfair to claim that all businesspersons, all corporate executives, or all Republicans have been enlisted in the Regressive Revolution. Many persons in those categories are profoundly troubled by the excesses of both rhetoric and reactionary policy in the "conservative" onslaught. The vanguard of that onslaught espouses a credo of corporate chauvinism—an ideology of neo-Darwinism that amounts to a virtual theology of political economy, combining the political philosophy of Calvin Coolidge with the religious imperialism of William McKinley and the economic ethics of William Graham Sumner.

The diverse constituencies recruited for the Regressive Revolution guaranteed that there would be some differences of policy priorities and ideological nuances; generational conflicts between traditional conservatives and "neocons"; mutual discomfort shared by the radical Religious Right and its agnostic confederates in academe, the media, and business. It was, first of all, the talent of William Buckley—and later, preeminently the gift of Ronald Reagan—to forge sufficient unity among these disparate groups to make the Revolution so largely successful, at least in its ascension to power and antiwelfare state agenda.

It has not always been easy to discern which component of the Regressive Revolution has been dominant, even in particular cases: the political and economic philosophies of scholars and journalists, or evangelical extremism, or cultural reaction (especially in matters of race and sex), or anticommunism, or ultranationalism, or commercial self-interest—or political opportunism exploiting all of the above.

Authoritarian Populism

A basic strategy of the Regressive Revolution has been to alienate the white middle class and workers from the federal government by playing on their concerns for economic security, family well-being, and "traditional values," often with large doses of religious rhetoric. This strategy foments an oxymoronic "authoritarian populism"—a demagogic manipulation of popular discontent in the service of oligarchic interests. It has succeeded dramatically in shifting the terms of public debate onto the platform of corporate self-aggrandizement. As a matter of fact, however, almost every candidate for the presidency for three decades (including Jimmy Carter and Bill Clinton) has resorted to populist anti-Washington rhetoric. Bill Clinton's 1996 State of the Union Address repeatedly (and falsely) promised that "the age of big government is over." This relentless demeaning of the federal government and of proper national responsibilities has made the actual conduct of government and the public understanding thereof increasingly problematic. But it is a game that, whatever the motives of its different players, can only reinforce the Business Mystique and the privatization of religious piety.

Ideology and Oligarchy

Three superb chroniclers of this regressive onslaught, writing at seven-year intervals, are Peter Steinfels, *The Neoconservatives: The Men Who Are Changing America's Politics* (1979); Sidney Blumenthal, *The Rise of the Counter-Establishment: From Conservative Ideology to Political Power* (1986); and Gary Dorrien, *The Neoconservative Mind* (1993).[1]

In 1979, as neoconservative momentum was growing during the faltering Carter administration, Steinfels opened his book with these words: "A distinct and powerful political outlook has recently emerged in the United States. . . . [T]his outlook, preoccupied with certain aspects of American life and blind or complacent toward others, justifies a politics which, should it prevail, threatens to attenuate and diminish the promise of American democracy."[2] Then, in the final paragraph of his book, Steinfels observed that the great danger posed by neoconservatism "is that it will become nothing more than the legitimating and lubricating ideology of an oligarchic America where essential decisions are made by corporate elites, where great inequalities are rationalized by straitened circumstances and a system of meritocratic hierarchy, and where democracy becomes an occasional, ritualistic gesture."[3]

By 1986, Blumenthal was able to document more fully the institutional bases and strategies of the conservative revolt: a "counter-establishment" of "factories of ideology," including think tanks (the American Enterprise

Institute, the Heritage Foundation, the Manhattan Institute, the Committee on the Present Danger, the Ethics and Public Policy Center); funding networks (Olin Foundation, Smith-Richardson Foundation, Richard Mellon Scaife, Coors Breweries, prime military contractors); advocacy journalists (in such media as *The Wall Street Journal*); ideological journals (*National Review, Commentary, The Public Interest*); and ideological television (beginning with William Buckley's "Firing Line" but expanding to an imperious aggregation of conservative forums on various networks).

Money in the War of Ideas

What is the role of money, Big Money, in the Regressive Revolution? It is huge. Inordinate. Fundamentally antidemocratic. Often decisive in particular campaigns or policy battles. Too often dispensed for the fabrication of "facts" in recounting the record of government, in attacking the character and viewpoints of opponents, in dehumanizing foreign "enemies." Money has become the indispensable basic weapon for the waging of ideological warfare in an age when the myriad political technologies are enormously expensive.

Most obviously, Big Money fuels political campaigns—especially their great television and radio costs—and fuels political opposition to effective limits on campaign finance.

Big Money also establishes quasi-political bases in higher education through corporate-funded policy institutes and endowed professorships at universities and colleges, with the clear (or covert) intention of promoting ideological correctness. Such ventures are part of the wide-ranging conservative (especially neoconservative) assault on the alleged liberal, socialist, feminist, anti-Western, multicultural forces said to be dominating and perverting higher education.

Most significantly, if less conspicuously, Big Money establishes and sustains nonacademic think tanks and their multi-institutional strategy to control political culture and public policy. Basic to that strategy is the think tanks' management of multiple outlets through the media and all other value-shaping institutions, including religion, education, and government itself. It is particularly these conservative and neoconservative think tanks that, since the late 1970s, have seized the initiative in public policy from the political parties, the gridlocked Congress, and the executive bureaucracies. Big Money recruits large legions of intellectual mercenaries, writers, and support staffs to wage the war of ideas, free from the constraints of academic peer review and faculty accountability. Big Money funds their computerized databases, communications, and mailing operations. Big Money supports the publication of their policy tracts and handbooks regularly distributed to members of Congress and their staffs. Big Money establishes new journals with dependable political viewpoints. Big Money publishes and circulates books to colleges and public schools. Big Money finances the relentless cultivation of both the print and broadcast media to capture Op-Ed space and talk-show time.

From their recruited legions, the think tanks provide a ready supply of personnel for numberless legislative and executive staff positions. At a meeting of Washington area political scientists in December 1980, an official of the American Enterprise Institute (AEI) claimed two remarkable achievements: (1)AEI had become an objective, nonpartisan center for distinguished scholars; and (2) over half of AEI's scholars were then serving on transition teams for the incoming Reagan administration. (The dissonance between these claims struck the audience if not the speaker.) Among AEI persons subsequently named to key administration posts were Jeane Kirkpatrick, ambassador to the United Nations; Murray Weidenbaum, chairman of the Council of Economic Advisers; James E. Miller III, chairman of the Federal Trade Commission, then director of the Office of Management and Budget; Richard Perle, assistant secretary of Defense; Michael Novak, delegate to the Conference on Security and Cooperation in Europe.

Where does the Big Money come from? Direct corporate and personal gifts provide a large share of think-tank income. But a special sustaining role is performed by several ideologically committed foundations. Throughout the 1980s, the Smith-Richardson Foundation, Olin Foundation, and Scaife Foundation each dispensed at least several million dollars annually to right-wing think tanks. In 1993, for more recent examples, such foundations gave $3.4 million to the American Enterprise Institute and $3.7 million to the Heritage Foundation, the two most influential Washington-based think tanks spearheading the Regressive Revolution.[4]

The Business Mystique and the Christian Right

Big Money, through these multiple institutional channels, has intensified the ideological struggle in ways that stimulate the most regressive impulses in American religious life. By playing on the myths of the Puritan Ethos and Agrarian Fundamentalism, and by spurious commitments to populism and individualism, moneyed interests have once again made the tenets of the Business Mystique seem core articles of Christian faith.

Since 1980, the Regressive Revolution has been remarkably successful in shaping a common agenda for the profits of corporations and presumed principles of Christian morality. The main connection is the claim that the federal government is the enemy of both business and religion: government programs and regulations undermine both economic growth and traditional family values. So the Christian Right, many of whose followers are persons of modest means, is enlisted in support of business elites.

James Davison Hunter's account of contemporary "culture wars" observed that "underlying the reverential endorsement of capitalism among these Evangelicals is the conviction that economic and spiritual freedoms go hand in hand, that one is impossible without the other." Among the most prominent Evangelical theologians,

> the celebration of capitalism—the freedom to pursue economic gain without government interference—is virtually unqualified. Jerry Falwell repeatedly claimed that "God is in favor of freedom, property, ownership, competition, diligence, work and acquisition. All of this is taught in the Word of God, in both the Old and New Testaments. . . . The free enterprise system is clearly outlined in the Book of Proverbs in the Bible. Jesus Christ made it clear that the work ethic was part of His plan for man. . . . Competition in business is biblical."

Similarly, religious broadcaster, former presidential candidate, and founder of the Christian Coalition Pat Robertson has declared that "free enterprise is the economic system most nearly meeting humanity's God-given need for freedom. . . . Capitalism satisfies the freedom-loving side of humanity."[5]

The Moral Majority (which succumbed after a raucous short life in the 1980s) and the Christian Coalition (which more shrewdly captured many of the town and county precincts of the Republican Party in the 1990s) are only the most obvious examples of religious co-optation by corporate economic interests. In the case of the Moral Majority, television preacher Jerry Falwell was directly solicited by direct-mail wizard Richard Viguerie, on behalf of the National Conservative Political Action Committee (NCPAC), and Paul Weyrich, co-founder of the right-wing Heritage Foundation, to enlist the televangelist constituency for conservative Republican politics. Thus the Moral Majority was formed in 1979 and became a major partner in Ronald Reagan's first election and early legislative victories. When Falwell's leadership faltered through recklessly extremist rhetoric and weak grassroots organization, the Moral Majority expired in 1989. That demise helped the Religious Right to make a new start with more political sophistication, especially in grassroots organizing. The Christian Coalition, strategically managed by a youthful Ralph Reed, forged effective alliances with Republican congressional leaders and bridged the hiatus between the economic agenda and the cultural agenda of disparate conservatives. (The connections between the Christian Coalition's "Contract with the American Family" and Speaker Newt Gingrich's "Contract with America" are discussed at the end of this chapter.)

The rank and file of the Religious Right have been particularly susceptible to the economic buccaneers' pretense that the conservative revival is more about culture—faith, flag, family, sex—than about the economy: a highly successful, pious distraction.

Think Tanks and the Rewriting of History

What the most aggressive and regressive conservatives have unabashedly celebrated is the theme and title of a nearly forgotten 1948 book by Richard Weaver, *Ideas Have Consequences*.[6] What they have unabashedly exploited is the discovery that, in late twentieth-century government, public policy has increasingly involved a political struggle over the manipulation of complex historical, social, and economic data—and the ideas that interpret them. At their most mischievous, think-tank warriors have specialized in fabricating wholesale mythologies about the histories of social and economic policy, the arms race, the diplomatic record, and the social witness of the churches and the ecumenical movement. George Orwell's *1984* anticipated these fabrications by portraying the annihilation of the distinction between reality and unreality through "the ceaseless retrospective rewriting of history."[7]

Politics in America has become something much more than a contest over the shaping of the future: It is a bitter conflict over stories of the past that define present reality—and unreality.

Central to the propaganda of the Regressive Revolution is a mythology of the almost total failure of modern American government and an inflammatory paranoia about government itself as the enemy of the people. Rather than providing a positive philosophy of the responsibilities of government, this revolution has waged a permanent campaign against government itself. The Business Mystique in America runs counter to the dominant business ideologies of Europe, especially in its historic account of the origins of the modern state. As Blumenthal puts it: "Whereas in Europe businessmen view the state as the creation of the aristocracy, American businessmen see the state as the creation of New Deal brain-trusters. In Europe, the state preceded the bourgeoisie; in America, businessmen consider the state a latecomer."[8]

"Statism"—especially as in "the welfare state"—became the cussword of conservative rhetoric. Antistatist, laissez-faire, fundamentalist, Social Darwinist tracts plunged the nation's public discourse back into the 1880s. In the early 1980s, however, these tracts purported to offer a new economic theology—"supply-side economics." Among its preachers were

Wall Street Journal editor Robert Bartley and writer Jude Wanniski; Irving Kristol, the "Godfather" of the neocons who did most to mobilize their funding and their front groups; economist Arthur Laffer; Congressman (later secretary of the Department of Housing and Urban Development [HUD] and vice presidential candidate) Jack Kemp. Their preachings, however, were not really new: glorification of the free market, reduced taxation, relaxed business regulation, a gospel that promised rapid economic growth, unprecedented prosperity, and—ultimately—more revenue for the government!

Jude Wanniski explained the history of this sacred doctrine to Ronald Reagan (who became an easy convert) in these mystifying testimonies to special providence:

> Supply-side's birth coincided with the birth of Christ and Christianity. It was Emperor Caesar Augustus who decided to revive the idea of his adoptive father Julius and conduct a tax census of the empire. By identifying the whole of the citizenry, the burden of taxes could be spread, avoiding the necessity of burdening the few with the entire load. Joseph and Mary were en route home to be enumerated for this supply-side economic purpose when Jesus was born.[9]

The economic core of this gospel would be decorously wrapped in a public theology of prayer, patriotism, optimism, and individualism—or, as Reagan himself preached it in his 1980 acceptance speech, "a community of shared values of family, work, neighborhood, peace, and freedom."

The Smith-Richardson Foundation (based on the fortunes of Vicks VapoRub) provided the funding for what its program officer, Leslie Lenkowsky, heralded as "the supply-side trilogy": Jude Wanniski's *The Way the World Works* (1978), George Gilder's *Wealth and Poverty* (1981), and Michael Novak's *The Spirit of Democratic Capitalism* (1982). Lenkowsky was candid about his foundation's ideological strategy:

> Supply-side economics is less an economic theory than a philosophy, an ideology. It's an effort to reorient policy. Foundations are not involved in politics directly. We're in the world of ideas. The kind of infrastructure we create is a network of people who know there is a place to go for funding and contacts. Primarily it's an educational process.[10]

While the right-wing think tanks were being lushly funded in the 1980s, their supply-side and extravagant military policies were actually *defunding* the United States government. During that decade, the national debt quadrupled. The United States was transformed from being the world's number one creditor nation to the world's number one debtor nation, more dependent than ever on foreign borrowing at high interest rates, thereby compounding the debt burdens and despair of the world's poorer countries. The slowdown of U.S. economic growth, the menacing specter of bankruptcy at all levels of government, and the recession at decade's end all contributed to the Republicans' loss of the White House in 1992 and hardened the hearts of many Americans against the supply-side gospel—at least temporarily.

Abolition of the Welfare State?

The social policies of the Reagan administration were charted by George Gilder's *Wealth and Poverty* (1981) in Reagan's first term and by Charles Murray's *Losing Ground: American Social Policy, 1950–1980* (1984) in the second term. Both Gilder and Murray were sustained at the Manhattan Institute, a conservative think tank founded by Wall Street lawyer and speculator, William Casey, Reagan's 1980 campaign chairman who became CIA director.

What Gilder, Murray, and other ideological point-men of the Regressive Revolution were doing was to overturn the claim of Daniel Bell, Seymour Martin Lipset, and the "end-of-ideology" camp of the early 1960s that conservatives had accepted the welfare state as a permanent reality. No more! These 1980s conservatives were *not* accepting the welfare state: they were determined to abolish it.

The antiwelfare state message of George Gilder had racial and sexist implications. According to Gilder:

> The worst contemporary tragedy . . . is the destruction of the black families of the inner cities, directly traceable to government programs. The worst experience for the black family since slavery has been the war on poverty. It was a catastrophe because it refused to acknowledge that family structures are essentially based on man the provider and woman the homemaker. Female-headed families are incapable of raising little boys, and they are incapable of escaping poverty under any circumstances.[11]

It was Gilder's purpose in *Wealth and Poverty* to "give capitalism a theology" of entrepreneurship that would bless the rich for "fostering opportunities for the classes below them in the continuing drama of the creation of wealth and progress."[12] Work, family, and faith were the sacred values trumpeted by Gilder, who wound up *Wealth and Poverty* with lyrics of love and individualism, "the endless dialogue between man and God, between alienation and providence, as we search for the ever-rising and receding promised land"—and finally with a familiar quotation from Reinhold Niebuhr, ending "Therefore we are saved by love."[13]

Charles Murray's *Losing Ground* claimed that New Deal and Great Society antipoverty programs had not only failed to help the poor but had made their lot even worse. Murray proposed saving social policy by killing it—eliminating almost all welfare for adults and all preferential treatment for minorities. He would do away with Aid to Families with Dependent

Children (AFDC), Medicaid, Food Stamps, Unemployment Insurance, Workers' Compensation, subsidized housing. In place of national welfare programs, Murray suggested that family members, friends, local charities, and the private job market should assume responsibility for needy persons. Such antigovernment, antiwelfare sentiments, echoed vociferously among congressional Republicans, drove the 1996 "welfare reform" that abandoned AFDC, cut Food Stamps, and devolved responsibility on the states and the private sector.

But, as T. S. Eliot once wrote, "the past has another pattern." The actual record of federal social policy can be recounted quite differently from Gilder's and Murray's accounts. Political scientist John Schwarz substantially challenged their versions in his *America's Hidden Success: A Reassessment of Twenty Years of Public Policy,* describing the years 1960 to 1980 as the most misinterpreted and undercredited period in governmental history. After reviewing a wide range of impact studies and census data, Schwarz found that government programs in that twenty-year period

> led to a diminishing of poverty among Americans by more than half. They significantly reduced flagrant malnutrition, lessened inequality in access to medical services, and were associated with dramatic declines in infant mortality rates among the poor and the minorities. They helped relieve overcrowded and substandard housing. They also improved the education of impoverished children and gave employable skills to thousands of otherwise unemployed adults.

Altogether, Schwarz concluded, those two decades provided "an age of distinguished public achievement."[14]

Moreover, as Michael Harrington, Warren Copeland, and others have pointed out, the full potential of the social policy initiatives of the 1960s was severely curtailed by the Vietnam War and its drain on leadership and budget.

The antiblack and antifeminist elements in the Regressive Revolution, whether blatant or sotto voce, were pinpointed by Allen Hunter in a 1987 lecture at the University of Wisconsin:

> Racial rhetoric links with anti-welfare state sentiments [and] fits with the push for economic individualism; thus many voters who say they are not prejudiced (and may not be by some accounts) oppose welfare spending as unjust. Anti-feminist rhetoric . . . is articulated around defense of the family, traditional morality, and religious fundamentalism.[15]

The antipathy to federal welfare programs has frequently indulged in stereotypical stories about black "welfare queens." Combined with federal retreats on civil rights and urban policy, the conservatives' escalation of antiwelfare sentiment exacerbated the racial separatism that has intensified since 1980.

That welfare policy itself needed reform had become a cliché of the 1980s and remained so in the 1990s. The hard political, and moral, question was whether governmental leadership could construct a program that would protect the well-being of poor children and disadvantaged parents by a better combination of financial support with adequate job training, employment opportunity, child care, and incentives to parental responsibility.

The neoconservative attack on government repeatedly claimed that the modern American state's social policies were fostering a demoralizing dependency, intruding on personal and private space, displacing the more proper functions of churches and voluntary associations, and generally dissolving the institutions of civil society, especially at the local community level. But two decades ago, social critic Sheldon Wolin offered a very different analysis of the forces destroying personal, family, and community relationships: the corporate and financial interests driving industrial production, technology, marketing, and nationalizing social systems, even while preaching an anachronistic gospel of individualism and local autonomy:

> The progress of power in America has had a special piquancy for the conservative. While conservative politicians composed hymnals to individualism, localism, Sunday piety, and homespun virtues, conservative bankers, businessmen, and corporate executives were busy devitalizing many local centers of power and authority, from the small business and family farm to the towns and cities. They created the imperatives of technological change and mass production which have transformed the attitudes, skills, and values of the worker; and erased most peculiarities of place, of settled personal and family identity; and made men and women live by an abstract time that is unrelated to personal experience or local customs.[16]

So Wolin characterizes one more case of the dismaying commonplaces of history—not only a gap but an absolute contradiction between an ideology and the social or political reality rationalized by that ideology, especially when economic interests are at stake. (But then that's what the Marxists always said!)

More recently, Gary Dorrien, analyzing the neoconservatives' attack on the state for its alleged encroachments on civil society, has written: "The problem was that civil society was undermined in America not only by the state, but more importantly by the market. Mediating structures [families, churches, voluntary associations] confronted not only the often overreaching arm of the modern bureaucratic state, but the relentlessly desacralizing and commodifying force of the market."[17]

The Regressive Revolution's homilies about "family values" tend to distract attention from the reality of increasing family distress in the face of business and financial trends promoted by the same revolution. Two decades after Sheldon Wolin's reference to the destructive impact of conservative and corporate forces on "personal and family identity," M.I.T. economist Lester Thurow observed: "Family values are under attack, not by government programs," but by "the economic system itself. . . . The one-earner middle-class family is extinct."[18]

The fierce political contest over who really promotes authentic family values and a vibrant civil society is now front-and-center in contemporary America. The neoconservatives' credentials for this confrontation are, to say the least, extremely suspect.

The Market and Health Care

For generations, free market ideology and its commodifying force have dominated this nation's increasingly chaotic institutional arrangements for health care. Although the Regressive Revolution's efforts to dismantle the welfare state amounted to repudiation of a half century of established public policy, the case of national health policy involved a very different dynamic, though the ideological basis was essentially the same. There has never been an established national responsibility for health care: no comprehensive system of health insurance, no recognition of health care as a human right or entitlement, no effective regulation of the medical-industrial complex and its economic costs, which during the 1980s first surpassed escalating military expenditures and then rose to four times the defense budget by the mid-1990s. This lack of policy, perpetuating the most massive nonsystem among the nation's basic institutions, pointed to a political fact of great human import: the United States, alone among Western industrial democracies, never really finished the construction of a welfare state.

There was a moment back in 1935, as the Social Security system was being designed, when a system of national health insurance was seriously discussed, but was then postponed to a more opportune political season. Throughout the subsequent six decades, that opportunity has been persistently frustrated by the medical-industrial complex, perhaps the most powerful parapolitical force in the country. In fact, no area of domestic policy has been more ideologically driven than health care, given the medical-hospital-private insurance stakes in free enterprise.

Throughout the 1960s and 1970s, a succession of commissions and task forces documented the mounting "health care crisis": the tens of millions of citizens without health insurance, the "can't-take-it-with-you" loss of insurance for persons losing or changing jobs, the runaway costs, the wasteful competition and duplication among high-tech hospitals, the drive toward more lucrative medical specialties at the expense of primary and preventive care, the regressive insurance taxes, the more-and-more monumental paperwork. More than twenty national insurance bills were introduced into the Congresses of the 1970s, but the more opportune political season failed to materialize. The resistance to "socialized medicine" on the part of the medical profession and the health insurance industry was still too formidable.

With Ronald Reagan's 1980 election to the presidency on an antigovernmental platform, virtually all serious political action for health care reform ceased. Government responsibility for health insurance was repudiated by all the ideological cohorts of the Reagan administration. The nation's churches, which had long been active advocates for such reform, gave up the effort. The only alternative seemed to be some proposal for promoting competition among private insurance plans. And that pointed toward the Clinton administration's "managed competition" plan that went down to defeat in 1994, after the President and Hillary Clinton declined to offer a government-run single-payer system. The Health Insurance Association of America, with its "Harry and Louise" television spots, surfaced as the most conspicuous ideological antagonist to basic change. The more opportune political season for comprehensive health care reform now seems away off again, although Congress in 1996 did enact a law providing for the "portability" of health insurance for persons changing or losing jobs.

The Market and Public Education

The antistatist ideology of the Regressive Revolution has been directed with particular militancy toward public education. In addition to the Religious Right's familiar battles to "get God back in the schools" through prayer amendments and the teaching of creationist theology— and to get sex education *out* of the schools—the neoconservatives have deepened the conflict ideologically. They have campaigned for a greater emphasis on free market principles and the virtues of competitiveness, and for the exposure of the alleged socialist and liberal ideas, in school curricula and textbooks. They have attacked the federal government's role in education, including the effort to define national standards, and have urged the abolition of the U.S. Department of Education. They have challenged the state's presumed monopoly of elementary and secondary education and have aggressively promoted voucher plans and tax credits to give parents "freedom of choice" to help fund private schools, proposals guaranteed to intensify both religious and racial separatism. Similarly, the privatization of public education in distressed inner cities—turning over the management of schools to profit-making private businesses—has begun to catch on as an alternative to underbudgeted public schools, while also raising inflammatory questions of racial politics and restraints on citizen participation.

Something more than educational philosophy and economic doctrine, then, is manifestly at stake in the regressive assault on public education. Racial, cultural, and gender issues are pressed with special vehemence in policy tracts, journal columns, and talk shows. Among the prime targets are affirmative action ("reverse discrimination"), bilingualism, multiculturalism (said to undermine national unity and what Norman Podhoretz called "a reverence toward Western civilization that was nothing short of religious in its intensity"), and feminism (the cause, charged Podhoretz, of "a vast wreckage of broken and twisted lives").[19]

For those who share the normative American tradition that public education is the most vital cultural institution for the cultivation and preservation of democracy—"the most legitimate engine of government," said Thomas Jefferson—this right-wing campaign to devitalize, delegitimize, and privatize public education is especially lamentable. It is all the more so at a time when the cultural and racial diversity of the nation is once again increasing dramatically.

The Market and Cities

The antistatist drives of the Regressive Revolution have hit the nation's central cities with devastating force. In the 1980s context—supply-side tax policies, booming defense spending, exploding budget deficits—social policy, and especially urban policy, was severely crippled. As a Ford Foundation study found at decade's end, the nation's "social deficits" were even more serious than its fiscal deficits.[20] The combined impacts of curbs on welfare and antipoverty programs, the resolute resistance to a national health security policy, and the assault on the public schools have compounded the systemic ills that continue to demoralize and destroy urban core communities. And the primary victims are the racial and ethnic minorities that are actually majorities in those communities.

But there is an older, deep-rooted ideological syndrome about American cities themselves that frustrates almost all impulses to transform urban life. In part, that syndrome reflects the persistence of an antiurban bias grounded in preindustrial Jeffersonian prejudices and Agrarian Fundamentalism. That bias in recent decades has been seriously tainted with racist attitudes and Republican partisanship. Perhaps most serious is the dogma that *the American city is primarily an economic entity, a marketplace* that exists for the production of wealth. Moreover, a city is not primarily a community at all, nor a *polis,* nor a cultural center, nor an educational center, nor a religious center. A city is therefore a creature of capitalist enterprise. It exists to promote and protect wealth. Wealth is produced primarily by technological development. The best institution for producing wealth and technological development is the modern corporation. The most important role of government in urban America is to promote investments that strengthen the market.

Given that ideological posture, the presumption of the proper approach to urban poverty and welfare has been to promote business, investment, and economic growth, promising that their benefits will trickle down to residential neighborhoods, produce jobs, and improve the lot of the poor. Urban policy should be a partnership between government and private enterprise, a partnership in which government provides incentives (especially tax breaks for business) to attract investments in the city—or so the rationale has been for many years.

These ideological presumptions about cities have been more or less shared by both Democratic and Republican administrations since the 1940s. But the reality is that the most trumpeted urban policies, like the "urban renewal" of the 1950s and 1960s, have done more for business than for the renewal of neighborhoods and urban living generally—and that private business has been unwilling to invest in areas of most critical need in most older cities, no matter how generous the incentives.

The Carter administration promised the nation's "first coherent urban policy." However, the resulting March 1978 document, *A New Partnership to Conserve America's Communities,* did not really offer an ideological alternative. That document's most innovative and most costly proposals—a national urban development bank, infrastructure public works, and an Urban Volunteer Corps—were not vigorously pressed upon Congress, which thereupon failed to act on them. Carter's attempts both to increase military spending and to balance the budget meant that cities were subjected to cuts in revenue sharing; reduced grants for mass transit, jobs programs, economic development, parks, and environmental protection; and reduced loans for home rehabilitation and small businesses.

In the 1980s, the Reagan administration set about to dismantle urban policies and programs. The emphasis was on getting the federal government out of social problems and urban services, and fervently promoting privatization and voluntarism. Block grants were shifted from cities to state governments increasingly controlled by suburban interests. Tax burdens were shifted from national to local and state governments, resulting in more regressive taxation particularly devastating to cities (notably property and sales taxes). The parade of bankruptcies and near-bankruptcies in cities, counties, and states has woefully punctuated both the fiscal and social deficits in this richest of all nations. The HUD budget of $36 billion in 1980 (amounting to 7 percent of the federal budget) was slashed to $15 billion by 1987 (amounting then to less than 2 percent of the budget). The scandals of entrepreneurial corruption in the Reagan administration's curtailed HUD budget further shortchanged the legitimate needs of cities. That corruption itself became the excuse for still further cuts.

The deregulation of many enterprises and the lax regulation of urban savings-and-loans multiplied taxpayer burdens into the hundreds of billions of dollars, and that by an antitax administration! In the same decade that the luxury housing market badly overexpanded, urban homelessness increased to Depression levels. Under the McKinney (Homeless) Act of 1987, a Special Needs Assistance Program was established to help with shelters, transitional housing, and housing amenities for the handicapped, but the grant total each year has been meager—amounting to a small fraction of the cost of one B-2 bomber. The Bush administration and congressional conservatives since 1989 have pushed for an end to all federal funding for urban mass transit and Amtrak subsidies.

Privatization thus continues to be a main drive of government policies affecting cities. The hard question remains: Will private capital ever meet public interests and needs adequately, as well as the most elemental needs of poor and marginalized people, in city, town, or country? If not, who or what will?

The Contract with America

The Regressive Revolution was briefly blunted by Bill Clinton's election in 1992. For two years, however, the Clinton administration's uncertain course between economic centrism and cultural liberalism helped set the stage for the Republicans' 1994 capture of both houses of Congress for the first time since 1952. That electoral victory was spurred by an unprecedented congressional campaign platform, titled "Contract with America" and signed by 367 Republican candidates for the House of Representatives six weeks before the election. Spearheaded by the House Speaker-to-be, Congressman Newt Gingrich of Georgia, the "Contract with America" provided congressional Republicans with a tight right-wing ideological coherence rare in American political history and a ten-point platform they promised to act on "within the first hundred days of the 104th Congress." Their strong sense of mandate was reinforced by the remarkable fact that not one single incumbent Republican in the House or Senate, or in any governorship, was defeated in that 1994 election.

If the Reagan years represented the first successful stage of the Regressive Revolution, the Gingrich years seemed to promise the second stage and a further swing to the Right. The "Contract with America" combined fiscal conservatism with corporate indulgence, punitive welfare policies, vengeful crime laws, and an anti-UN act. Wrapped in euphemistic rhetoric, the main benefits to business were disguised by the very titles of the ten planks in the platform. For instance, "The Job Creation and Wage Enhancement Act" was not really about workers but about capital gains tax cuts, business incentives, the deregulation of corporations, and cuts in estate taxes. "The Common Sense Legal Reforms Act" included "loser pays" laws deterring litigation against corporations concerning product liability, discrimination, and sexual harassment.

The rhetoric of "reform" was particularly misappropriated with regard to budget and welfare issues. Although a proposed balanced budget amendment to the Constitution was twice narrowly defeated in the Senate, Congress succeeded in pressuring Clinton to accept a seven-year Republican timetable for achieving a balanced budget. Both sides acquiesced in the folly of depriving the government of the capacity to borrow in times of severe economic distress or for prudent long-term planning. In 1996, Congress passed and Clinton approved a modified "Contract" budget-balancing proposal for "welfare reform" that promised to reduce spending by $55 billion over six years, terminated federal entitlements for poor children, shifted welfare funds to block grants to the states, required most adults to work within two years of receiving benefits, limited benefits to five years, and denied benefits to most legal immigrants not yet citizens.

In 1996, however, at least one political analyst predicted that the conservative surge would soon dissipate and be displaced by a "liberal revival." E. J. Dionne, Jr., a *Washington Post* columnist, based that prediction on evidence that the public was dismayed by 1995 and 1996 congressional actions to shut down the government, to weaken environmental protection, and to curtail Medicare. Newt Gingrich's meteoric rise seemed to reverse toward free fall, at least temporarily; his "negatives" in the polls rose rapidly. Dionne also noted public disgust with the way Republican presidential primaries got "bogged down in a swamp of negativism." He declared that "the time has come to junk the conventional wisdom about the inevitable triumph of the right" and to recognize that voters, "far from looking to tear government down, have for some years been hoping for a government that worked, that solved problems, that sought to improve average living standards." That is the perspective from which Dionne has also written a book optimistically titled *They Only Look Dead: Why Progressives Will Dominate the Next Political Era.*[21]

However, the mass exodus of liberal and moderate Democrats, and also of moderate Republicans, from Congress in 1996 suggested that many political veterans in both parties could foresee no such progressive future. Further doubt was cast by the many centrist-to-conservative planks in the Democrats' 1996 platform and by the priorities of Bill Clinton's reelection campaign.

The Christian Coalition and the Contracts

Signaling a new departure for right-wing evangelicals, Christian Coalition Executive Director Ralph Reed used the pages of the Heritage Foundation's journal *Policy Review* in the summer of 1993 to acknowledge that "the pro-family movement's political rhetoric has often been policy-thin and value-laden, leaving many voters tuned out." It was time, he wrote, for the profamily movement to "speak to the concerns of average voters in the areas of taxes, crime, government waste, health care and financial security." That announcement presaged the Christian Coalition's heavy involvement in 120 Republican congressional races in 1994 (with victories in the majority) and in Newt Gingrich's legislative campaigns for the "Contract with America." The thirty-four-year-old Reed was rewarded with the conspicuous presence of Speaker Gingrich, Senators Phil Gramm (Texas) and Majority Whip Trent Lott (Mississippi), and House Budget Chair John Kasich (Ohio) in the Mansfield Room of the Capitol on May 17, 1995, when the Christian Coalition presented its "Contract with the American Family" to a televised news conference. "We have finally gained what we have always sought," said Reed. "A place at the table, a sense of legitimacy and a voice in the conversation that we call democracy."[22]

The ten-point "Contract with the American Family" was a cultural and moral gloss on the "Contract with America" that tended to obscure the economic interests at stake. Among the provisions of the Coalition's "Contract":

> Allow communal prayer in public schools and courthouses
> Abolish the U.S. Department of Education
> Establish vouchers for private and parochial schools
> Favor a flat tax "in concept"
> Mandate strict limits on abortion
> Curb pornography on cable television and the Internet
> Abolish federal funding for the National Endowments for the Arts and Humanities, the Corporation for Public Broadcasting, and the Legal Services Corporation for poor people

Turn over welfare programs to private charities

Reject the United Nations Convention on the Rights of the Child

Require prisoners to study and work, and require restitution to victims subsequent to prisoners' release

Seldom if ever in American history has there been such a strategic mutual co-optation between a national political party and a professedly Christian organization. And, like almost all the nominally Christian political parties of Europe and Latin America, this alliance too is a decidedly conservative one. Critics charged idolatry.

6

THE REGRESSIVE REVOLUTION II: ANTICOMMUNISM AND AFTER

Neoconservatism is the final stage of the Old Left, the only element in American politics whose identity is principally derived from its view of Communism. Like the conservatives, the neoconservatives depend upon their enemy for their own definition. . . . Neoconservatives [believe] that liberals are either a species of Stalinist fellow traveler or operate "objectively" . . . in the broad interest of the Soviet Union.

—Sidney Blumenthal,
The Rise of the Counter-Establishment

This is the *negative face* of moral conflict: the deliberate, systematic effort to discredit the opposition. In the culture war, this negative aspect of the conflict has taken on a life and force of its own; indeed, neutralizing the opposition through a strategy of public ridicule, derision, and insult has become just as important as making credible moral claims for the world that each side champions.

—James Davison Hunter,
Culture Wars

Nothing provided more ideological cohesion among the varieties of conservatives and neoconservatives in the Regressive Revolution than a militant, chauvinistic anticommunism. The intellectual firepower of that brand of anticommunism (as distinct from the anti-Soviet "containment" views of such "political realists" as George Kennan, Hans Morgenthau, and Reinhold Niebuhr) was initially provided by several repentant excommunists. These were men who had turned sharply to the Right in the 1960s—men like New York philosophers Sidney Hook and James Burnham, veterans of the ideological warfare of the 1930s. Both would be awarded the Medal of Freedom by President Reagan in the 1980s, although Hook soon afterward reproached Reagan for "going soft on communism."

What Hook, Burnham, and other erstwhile leftists nurtured in a new generation of rightists was the predatory invective of their former Marxist-Leftist polemics—a rhetorical style that was vicious, vindictive, derisive, and just plain mean. That style came to mark the neoconservative movement among journalists, think-tankers, and even theologians from the 1970s through the 1980s and into the 1990s. It is a style, as Gary Dorrien put it, that is "less interested in promoting dialogue with opponents than with demolishing them."[1] It is a style that has invaded not only the political arena but also the universities and the churches. By the mid-1990s, the raucous decline of civility in public discourse had itself become a major topic of public discourse—not that the neocons should be charged with a monopoly of meanness. There tends to be a spiral in vicious public rhetoric in which most, if not all, the antagonists get caught. (Only a very few of us seem capable of perfect charity and rationality and decency at all times.)

From Left to Right

Whatever the inheritance of the Regressive Revolution from the communist polemics of the 1930s, many of the bellwethers of the New Right in the 1970s and after were converts from the New Left and liberal sectors of the 1960s. But prominent among these bellwethers were sociologists Daniel Bell and Seymour Martin Lipset, who, having declared "the end of ideology" in the 1950s and 1960s, resurfaced as neocons in the 1970s. And it was a former schoolmate of Bell and Lipset at New York's City College, Irving Kristol, who in the 1970s first claimed the label "neoconservative" for himself—long after an earlier identity as a communist of the Trotskyite variety. It was Irving Kristol who, having metamorphosed into a registered Republican and adviser to President Nixon, became the neoconservatives' "Godfather," unabashedly declaring: "I raise money for conservative think tanks. I am a liaison . . . between intellectuals and the business community."[2] Kristol brought to this role a career as a veteran anticommunist and political journalist, originally with the Jewish journal *Commentary,* later with *The Wall Street Journal* and the think-tank organs of the American Enterprise Institute and other neoconservative institutes.

Norman Podhoretz, editor of *Commentary* beginning in 1960, pontificated in his first decade as a utopian, countercultural New Leftist opposed to nuclear weapons and the Vietnam War. Not long after, he too made the big move from Left to Right. So alienated did he become from the peace, civil rights, and feminist movements—and from virtually all forms of liberalism and détente—that near the end of Jimmy Carter's first year in the White House, Podhoretz would write an essay for *Harper's* titled "The Culture of Appeasement." That title became a main theme for *Commentary,* no longer a left-liberal journal but one of the shrillest and most influential voices of neoconservatism. In 1980, Podhoretz published a volume similarly titled *The Present Danger: Do We Have the Will to Reverse the Decline of American Power?* And that title traded on the name of the Committee on the Present Danger, which Podhoretz helped found and which sounded the false alarm that the Soviet Union had achieved military superiority with the buildup of its nuclear arsenal. (The reality of the 1970s was that the United States increased its potential nuclear targets in the Soviet Union from about 1,700 to over 9,000, while pursuing all the new counterforce technologies: cruise missiles, Mark 12-A warheads, Trident missiles and submarines, Pershing II rockets, MX missiles. At decade's end, the United States possessed thousands more strategic nuclear weapons than the Soviet Union.)

Two veteran officials of former Democratic administrations, Eugene Rostow and Paul Nitze, became the main standard-bearers of the Committee on the Present Danger; then they would become the Reagan administration's top officials in nuclear arms talks. Reagan also named Podhoretz chairman of an advisory committee for the U.S. Information Agency. Podhoretz's son-in-law, thirty-three-year-old Elliott Abrams, was appointed assistant secretary of state for Latin America, from which post he managed the Reagan administration's interventionist policies in Nicaragua and other Central American countries. Abrams' illegal solicitations of donations to keep the Contras' warfare going and "his dissembling appearances before congressional committees later provided some of the Iran-Contra scandal's most bizarre material. Abrams subsequently pleaded guilty to two counts of a plea-bargained federal indictment for his attempts to deceive congressional committees."[3] In 1996, he became president of one of the most prominent think tanks long engaged in right-wing attacks on the mainline churches and the ecumenical movement, the Ethics and Public Policy Center (which will be treated in the next chapter).

By 1986, Norman Podhoretz was savagely rebuking President Reagan for having become a "Carter clone" in seeking arms agreements with the Soviets. One of Podhoretz's allies in both nuclear and Central American affairs was the hawkish and politically ambitious president of ideologically embattled Boston University, John Silber, who would later wage a losing campaign for the governorship of Massachusetts. In 1989, of all years—the year of Eastern Europe's "velvet revolutions" and the collapse of the Berlin Wall—Texan Silber published a haplessly ill-timed book titled *Straight Shooting*. That alarmist screed echoed Podhoretz in imagining that Reagan's "appeasement" of Mikhail Gorbachev was akin to Neville Chamberlain's appeasement of Adolf Hitler at Munich in 1938. "President Reagan may now go down in history as the man who undermined the NATO alliance and weakened beyond repair the bonds tying the Federal Republic of Germany to the West"—all of which, according to Silber, was leading to "a *Pax Sovietica* in which the free world will have become an illusion."[4] Within two years, the Soviet Union ceased to exist and the former East Germany was incorporated into NATO.

The attacks on Reagan by such as Podhoretz and Silber indicated that even zealous anticommunism could not always guarantee unity among the right-wing legions.

Who Lost the Cold War?

By 1991, the Cold War was over. Now many right-wingers rallied to the claim that Ronald Reagan's "peace through strength" military policies had won the Cold War. Central to that claim was the notion that Reagan's nuclear arms buildup and, more especially, his "Strategic Defense Initiative" (SDI; a.k.a. "Star Wars") had trumped the Soviet military and exhausted the Soviet economy. Neither Pentagon scientists nor Congress's Office of Technology Assessment had imagined that strategic missile defense was technologically feasible, let alone dreamed that "Star Wars" weapons would, as Reagan promised, render "nuclear weapons impotent and obsolete." Actually, the idea of "Star Wars" defense was a think-tank fantasy birthed at the Heritage Foundation at the instigation of Edward Teller, father of the hydrogen bomb, and Lieutenant General Daniel Graham, former head of the Defense Intelligence Agency. Financial support for the idea's development came from the Olin Foundation and such pro-Reagan Sunbelt industrialists as Joseph Coors and Justin Dart. *The Wall Street Journal* offered editorial support. The stakes for industry might be enormous: former Secretary of Defense James Schlesinger estimated the possible ultimate costs at $1 trillion, which would make SDI the single most costly project ever undertaken by any government. Norman Podhoretz insisted that the "Star Wars" strategy "really does hold out the rational hope of an eventual escape from the threat of nuclear war."[5]

But was it "Star Wars" and the nuclear buildup of the Reagan administration that ended the Cold War and gave America the victory?

From 1983 on, Reagan and his early policies faced mounting pressures from concerned NATO governments, the antinuclear movements in both Europe and the United States, the critical engagement of the prestige professions (scientists, physicians, lawyers), the nearly unanimous opposition from the leaders of national Christian and Jewish bodies, the resistance of the Democratic Congress, runaway budget deficits generated by the failure of "supply-side" tax policies and by military profligacy, and the looming prospect (to the reported dismay of Nancy Reagan) that Ronald Reagan would be historically condemned for his failures to be a peacemaker.

It was in the context of these political and personal pressures on Reagan that Mikhail Gorbachev's *glasnost, perestroika*, and relentless disarmament initiatives brought the two superpower leaders together for four summit conferences, an intermediate nuclear forces (INF) treaty, and the actual beginnings of strategic arms reductions (START). Gorbachev helped redeem Reagan's place in history; Reagan helped assure Gorbachev's 1990 Nobel Peace Prize and altogether unique place in the history of the twentieth century.

But on the ground, beneath the high-level diplomacy of the superpowers, other extraordinary, nonmilitary powers were shaking the foundations of communist tyranny. In almost all the countries of Eastern Europe, Christian leaders and their churches were decisively involved in the miraculous events of 1989.

In Poland, following a decade of the church-supported Solidarity movement of Lech Walesa, a devout Roman Catholic editor became prime minister. Then Walesa himself became president.

In East Germany, the Protestant churches, whose prayer meetings for some years had nurtured a peace movement, now provided forums for political dialogue and dissent that overflowed into the streets with massive peaceful demonstrations. The crowds sang "We Shall Overcome." First Erich Honecker, then one communist leader after another, yielded the powers of Marxist-Leninist control. For a time, a coalition cabinet included three clergy (one of whom, a conscientious objector, held the incredible portfolio of "Minister of Defense *and* Disarmament").

In Czechoslovakia, the "Velvet Revolution" featured a philosophically minded playwright, Vaclav Havel, whose imprisonment for his political courage in support of human rights had provided an interval for spiritual transformation. In 1989, fulfilling the promise of his 1979 essay titled "The Power of the Powerless," the prisoner became president and attended a Catholic Mass as his first public act. For six months, the new deputy prime minister was the head of the Evangelical Church of Czech Brethren.

In Romania, a courageous Reformed pastor in Timisoara, Laszlo Tokes, inspired a huge crowd of protectors among Reformed and Orthodox believers following his protests against the inhumanities of Ceausescu's barbaric dictatorship. Within days (though not without bloodshed), the barbaric dictator himself was deposed and dead.

In the Soviet Union, in the wake of the irresistible 1988 celebrations of the millennium of Russian Christianity, the government of Mikhail Gorbachev turned to the churches for moral and practical support in the "spiritual" struggle for *perestroika* (reconstruction). In turn, the churches gained their freedom, new opportunities, and heavy responsibilities.

And in Hungary, at the strong urging by both Catholic and Protestant leaders, the communist government opened its frontier with Austria, thus allowing tens of thousands of East German emigrés to pass through on the way to West Germany. This hemorrhaging of the body politic was the final blow to the communist regime of the German Democratic Republic.

So the Wall came tumbling down.

Americans of all political affiliations and persuasions should therefore constrain the temptation to claim all the credit for the tumbling of the Wall. Millions of European Christians—and, yes, even some prudent communist leaders—should be generously remembered for their crucial roles in the dissolution of the Cold War blocs.

The subsequent disintegration of the Soviet Union and the downfall of Gorbachev reinforced, for at least a season or two, the triumphalist conviction that the United States had won the Cold War. But all too soon, it became apparent that there was much less cause for euphoria. The sudden collapse of Soviet authority created an array of daunting new problems. It disrupted effective Russian control over nuclear weapons, weapons-grade materials, and surplus nuclear scientists, thereby increasing the perils of nuclear proliferation and terrorism. In displacing Gorbachev for Boris Yeltsin, the Soviet collapse subjected Russian political life to erratic, mercurial leadership less dependably committed to the rule of law. And it subjected Russia and the other republics to economic and social chaos (including the collapse of "safety nets"), which, in turn, made their populaces more susceptible to extremist movements: ultra-nationalist, monarchist, anti-Semitic, and resurgent communists, all of whom sought to exploit popular distress and bitterness.

There is a still heavier accounting to be done regarding historic claims about the Cold War: the enormous costs on both sides meant that, in many respects yet to be fully measured, both the Soviet Union and the United States lost the Cold War. Former ambassador to Moscow George Kennan, dean of U.S. specialists in all things Russian, has soberly reflected on the ambiguous outcome of this half-century conflict:

> Nobody "won" the Cold War. It was a long and costly political rivalry, fueled on both sides by unreal and exaggerated estimates of the intentions and strength of the other side. It greatly overstrained the economic resources of both countries, leaving them both, by the end of the 1980s, confronted with heavy financial, social, and—in the case of the Russians—political problems neither had anticipated and for which neither was fully prepared. . . . All these developments should be seen as part of the price we are paying for the Cold War.[6]

The costs of the Cold War, when combined with the myopic domestic economic and social policies of the 1980s, account heavily for the "social deficits" reported by the Ford Foundation's 1989 study *The Common Good: Social Welfare and the American Future,* including the following: (1) Increasing millions of American children were impoverished, born out of wedlock, living with teenage mothers and/or homeless, receiving inadequate nutrition, preschool education, day care, and health care. (2) Millions of disadvantaged adolescents were caught in a pattern of poor schooling, dropping out, joblessness or low-pay dead-end jobs, and inadequate sex education. (3) Millions of American workers were slipping toward poverty with stagnant or declining wages (including regressive minimum wage levels), structural unemployment in a technology-driven global economy, and no health insurance.[7]

Such social deficits represent political and ideological deficits. They cannot fairly be limited to partisan or conservative defaults, but they were greatly exacerbated during the reactionary Cold War obsessions and the regressive tax and social policies of the Reagan regime.

Moreover, it was not only the Russians and the Americans who were heavy losers in the Cold War, nor just their bloc allies in Europe. The extension of the Cold War to Africa, Asia, and Latin America militarized and severely distorted the economic and political development of dozens of countries, making them "client states" of either the United States or the Soviet Union, and plunging many of them into civil strife. The Vietnam War and its expansion into Cambodia and Laos were only the most costly of many such conflicts. Preoccupied with waging their global conflict, the superpowers largely neglected the economic development policies that offered the greatest hope in overcoming poverty, hunger, and disease. Uncountable millions of Third World lives have been casualties of the Cold War, including—even in the 1990s—recurring victims of American and Russian weapons in the arsenals of warring tribes and factions in such countries as Somalia, Angola, and Afghanistan.

These unending costs of the Cold War ought to serve, much more than they do, as curbs on American triumphalism and as spurs to policies of repentance and reconstruction.

The Lost Cause

What the end of the Cold War has done to the Regressive Revolution, in particular, has been to deprive the varieties of conservatives and neoconservatives of their most agglutinative power—anticommunism. Soon after trumpeting the claim that they had won the Cold War, they had to acknowledge that they had lost their unifying cause. Gary Dorrien observed in 1993:

> The end of the Cold War magnified their disagreements and shattered their alliances. With the loss of the Right's anticommunist touchstone, the deepening splits within American conservatism and neoconservatism fanned liberal hopes that the Right was disintegrating. These splits were real—but so was the conservatism of America's mass political culture.[8]

Such liberal hopes were short-lived; the Republicans' ultraconservatives took over Capitol Hill the very next year.

The New Gospels of Globalization

The Gingrich-led Congress of 1995–1996, with its "Contract with America," helped to restore energy and cohesion on the Right, not only by intensifying its antistatist economic and social agenda but also by a new global ideology articulated most enthusiastically by Newt Gingrich himself. Eclipsing the negative tenets of anticommunism, Gingrich has advocated the aggressive global promotion of a futuristic brand of capitalism, based on a high-tech, information-based world economy. The futuristic thrust was inspired by the works of Alvin and Heidi Toffler, whose projection of the "Third Wave" of history is represented in a 1994 publication of Gingrich's own think tank, the Progress and Freedom Foundation, titled *Creating a New Civilization: The Politics of the Third Wave.* Gingrich's technocratic vision of globalization was most boldly set forth in his 1984 book, *Window of Opportunity.* That work abounds with optimism about the "transformational" promises of information technology, microelectronics, space exploration, satellites, and biotechnology.

But beneath the futuristic appeal of this high-tech vision of global capitalism lies the political philosophy that binds Gingrich to the Regressive Revolution—a reversion to a minimalist government of laissez-faire, a Social Darwinist revolt against the welfare state, and a new economic imperialism in foreign policy. This is a vision, as E. J. Dionne, Jr., puts it, that moves "back to the future." Dionne writes that "when Gingrich envisions the Republican Party as representing the forces of the future—those who are doing well in the new economy, or expect or hope to, and are therefore willing to take the risk of accelerating the transition into the Third Wave—he is consciously echoing the Republican gambit of William McKinley in 1896. . . . The 1896 Republicans had made a fundamental choice: to represent the rising forces of industrialism, to organize the emerging captains of industry as the party's financial arm and to write off the country's 'backward' rural sectors."[9] Gingrich clearly intends to represent the rising forces of global high-tech capitalism by reincarnating the Coolidge dictum that "the business of America is business." The Business Mystique lives on! Dionne again:

> This vision sees American progress as depending upon a large-scale dismantling of the federal apparatus, including functions related to welfare and income support, consumer and environmental protection, economic regulation and management. [Gingrich] is, as a matter of principle, unconcerned about rising income inequality created by the new economy because he is as unabashed as his 19th-century conservative forebears were in seeing rewards for the wealthy, the productive and the innovative as the key to technological advance and economic improvement. By tearing down governmental barriers to change, Gingrich believes, he will accelerate the

arrival of a high-tech information age with unparalleled possibilities for American society. By building a disciplined and highly competitive society, Americans will be able to leap into the global marketplace and fulfill their destiny of "leading the human race."[10]

Gingrich's regressive futurism was not exclusively economic. He joined fellow right-wingers in seeking to restore the "Star Wars" technologies projected in the Reagan years and also to increase military spending above the levels requested by the Pentagon. So the Cold War lives on, after all, in the minds of many.

Among the neoconservatives heralding a new democratic-capitalist globalism in the 1990s were columnist Charles Krauthammer and a trio at the American Enterprise Institute: Joshua Muravchik, Michael Novak, and Ben Wattenberg.

Krauthammer's vision of a new Pax Americana was based on the conviction that "global unilateralism is not really a choice; it is an existing reality." His ardor for exporting democracy combined with cynicism toward the United Nations, the World Court, and regional organizations like the Organization of American States.[11] For Muravchik, the promotion of democratic idealism required yet another military buildup to cope with three potential enemies in the post–Cold War period: "a Russia that reverts to dictatorship and militarism, a China that grows wealthy and imperious without growing free, and an Islamic world that becomes further infected with virulent extremism and secures weapons of mass destruction."[12] Novak's ardent universalism was rationalized by the confidence that "most of the world was tuning in to American culture and trying to emulate America's political and economic systems."[13] Wattenberg similarly proclaimed: "We are the first universal nation. 'First' as in the first one, 'first' as in 'number one.' And 'universal' within our borders and globally." Leading neocons had thus managed to shape a new, but old, ideological orientation to postcommunist foreign policy: missionary, probusiness, interventionist, and what Wattenberg exuberantly termed "Neo-Manifest Destinarianist."[14]

But American exceptionalism could still take an opposite, isolationist tack. Patrick Buchanan's more traditional conservatism and nativism led him to declare in 1990: "What we need is a new nationalism, a new patriotism, a new foreign policy that puts America first, and not only first, but second and third as well."[15] From that alternative America-Firstism, Buchanan could oppose the neocons' "messianic globaloney" as well as the United Nations and George Bush's Gulf War.

In the 1990s, the ideological question that pressed most severely on the former Soviet satellites of Central and Eastern Europe was whether there was any social vision beyond the collapse of Leninism and the resurgence of the American Business Mystique. "Market fundamentalism" tended to be the prime American export to that region, most of whose peoples were experiencing the hardships of economic dislocations, social strife, and the breakdown of welfare systems. As they discovered that the market alone offers an inadequate social vision, one country after another began to seek a new authoritarian refuge, in several cases returning communists to power.

One of the perils of the Regressive Revolution is that, for all its preachings about freedom, its own economic determinism has too much in common with the economic determinism of the Marxist-Leninists whom it professes to have overcome. The victims of oppression in both communist and capitalist systems would perhaps grasp this irony more readily than those systems' most sophisticated theorists.

7

CHURCHES IN THE IDEOLOGICAL STRUGGLE

The corporate community has replaced the church, the extended family and even the community as the transmitter of values and ethics.
—Gary Edward, quoted in Jones,
Capitalism and Christians

For about 25 years, strategists on the right in American politics have wedded "think tanks" and activist institutions to friendly foundations and corporations to wage what is widely termed "the war of ideas" and the "cultural war." . . . [The] consistent ideological attacks on the mainline churches are part of a larger strategy of assaulting institutions in the arts, education, labor and media as well as targeting such social issues as abortion and gay rights.

—Leon Howell,
Funding the War of Ideas

Churches, like individuals, are ideological creatures: inevitably, inescapably, and imperatively. Like individuals, churches typically try to deny that they have an ideology. Church-generated ideologies may be subconscious, unreflective, inarticulate, but they are nonetheless real.

When Pope John Paul II issues a 1991 encyclical, *Centesimus Annus,* on the hundredth anniversary of Leo XIII's landmark economic encyclical, *Rerum Novarum,* and the new encyclical largely discharges the state from primary responsibility for securing economic rights, urges governments to promote a "business economy" and eliminate the presumed "excesses" of the welfare state, and appeals for greater reliance on the works of voluntarism and charity—that is hardly a document devoid of ideology. It is a document the ideological themes of which have caused the encyclical to be enthusiastically embraced by the leading American neoconservatives. The American Enterprise Institute's Michael Novak, whose theological sacralization of capitalism won praise from Ronald Reagan and Margaret Thatcher, was pleased at *Centesimus Annus*'s apparent dependence on his own writings: "I must say I'm quite gratified to see so many passages seeming to reflect from my own work. . . . I was very glad to see it given such a big megaphone."[1]

Remember the definition: an *ideology* is a set of beliefs and symbols that serve to interpret social reality and to motivate political action. The churches of Jesus Christ are, and in good faith ought to be, generating centers of beliefs and symbols that serve to interpret social reality and to motivate political action. That does not mean the churches should declare themselves officially to be either capitalist or socialist, Republican or Democrat. It does mean taking full account of the ways the churches' scriptures, teachings, pronouncements, publications, polities, bureaucratic structures, missional priorities, properties, and financial investments are all loaded with ideological content—not least when the churches pretend to be transcendent and nonpartisan in political and economic matters. And it means that the churches should engage their members in conscious, reflective, and articulate struggle over how best to interpret social reality and motivate political action.

Since the mid-1970s, the churches of the United States have been caught up in an ideological struggle of unprecedented intensity and increasing bitterness. Although many church leaders, both clergy and lay, have been painfully aware of this struggle, perhaps most church members have had little consciousness of the economic interests involved. Church leaders themselves have tended to lack a constructive strategy for involvement in the struggle.

Yet Hebrew and Christian scriptures are loaded with political and economic subject matter. From the prophet Amos to the prophet Jesus, the Bible speaks to the conduct of governments, the power of empires, the relationships between rich people and poor people, and the issues of violence and peace. Throughout the twentieth century, church bodies have addressed social, economic, and international problems and policies in social creeds, pronouncements, resolutions, encyclicals, pastoral letters, and testimony before government bodies. Inevitably and rightly, such messages have been controversial, both within the churches and in public debate. But most of the time, in principle, ecclesial messages on public issues have sought to disavow any ideological taint.

Think-Tank Theology and Corporate Warfare

What is remarkable about the past two decades of the inevitable encounter between religious and economic institutions is the aggressiveness of corporate business assault on the mainline churches, both Catholic and Protestant, and on ecumenical councils. That assault, however, is largely indirect, covert, and refracted through a variety of value-shaping institutions. It is heavily ideological. It has been primarily waged through an array of newly established (since 1975) corporate-funded think tanks with specifically religious and ethical agendas and with ambitious media strategies: notably the Ethics and Public Policy Center (1976), the Institute on Religion and Democracy (1981), and the Institute on Religion and Public Life (1990). The older American Enterprise Institute established its own department of religious studies in 1978.

The leaders of these institutions have all served in the front ranks of the Regressive Revolution. From their founding, their ideological affinities with such secular think tanks as the American Enterprise Institute, the Heritage Foundation, and the Manhattan Institute have been conspicuous and undeniable.

The three most prominent leaders of these ventures in the 1990s have happened to be Roman Catholics. Two are laymen: Michael Novak of the American Enterprise Institute, and George Weigel, until 1996 president of the Ethics and Public Policy Center (EPPC). The third is a former Lutheran pastor turned Catholic priest, Richard John Neuhaus, president of the Institute on Religion and Public Life. These three form an intimate, interlocking association of participation in each other's institutions. All three are unquestionably intelligent, articulate persons able to hold their own in both theological and public policy debates. They are nonetheless dependable servants of the corporate and foundation interests that finance their work. That is not necessarily a judgment about their motives; it is simply a comment about their ideological location and function. And they function as intellectual apologists—ideological recruits waging theological warfare in defense of corporate interests. Their soldiering for secular business values is particularly remarkable in view of their persistent laments about the alleged sway of secularism over religious values in American society.

The close affinity among this neoconservative threesome is even suggested in the titles of their publications: Novak's 1982 book, *The Spirit of Democratic Capitalism,* and its 1993 sequel, *The Catholic Ethic and the Spirit of Capitalism;* Weigel's 1990 essay, "American Catholicism and the Capitalist Ethic," in a volume edited by Peter Berger titled, *The Capitalist Spirit: Toward a Religious Ethic of Wealth Creation;* Neuhaus's 1992 book (dedicated to Peter and Brigitte Berger), *Doing Well and Doing Good: The Challenge to the Christian Capitalist.*[2]

Michael Novak's brief 1981 tract, *Toward a Theology of the Corporation,* prefigured his later, more substantial paeans to capitalism. Invoking the biblical image of the suffering servant, Novak portrayed the business corporation as the victim of "the anticapitalist bias of the Roman Catholic Church [before Pope John Paul II, that is], of major American and European theologians in this century, and of the pronouncements of the Protestant churches."[3]

For many years one of my favorite texts in scripture has been Isaiah 53:2–3: "He hath no form nor comeliness; and when we shall see him, there is no

71

beauty that we should desire him. He is despised and rejected of men; a man of sorrows, and acquainted with grief; he was despised, and we esteemed him not." I would like to apply these words to the modern business corporation, a much despised incarnation of God's presence in the world.[4]

Novak went on to identify "seven signs of grace in the corporation . . . a suitably sacramental number": creativity, liberty, birth and mortality, social motive, social character, insight, and the risk of liberty and election.[5] His emphasis on the social shape and the "inherent ideals" of corporations led him to exalt them above "the ideology of laissez-faire [and] the ideology of rugged individualism."[6] While acknowledging some exceptional moral deficiencies in some corporations, he insisted that "a theology of the corporation should attempt to show how corporations may be instruments of redemption, of humane purposes and values, of God's grace; it should also attempt to show their characteristic and occasional faults in every sphere."[7] For two decades, Novak has become increasingly enamored of the notion that business elites constitute the most "religious" of all vocations.

Novak's later works, especially *The Spirit of Democratic Capitalism* (1982) and *Will It Liberate? Questions About Liberation Theology* (1986), have offered sweeping critiques of Latin American liberation theology for its use of economic dependency theory and its alleged Marxist excesses against capitalism.[8]

Michael Novak's repudiation of radical theology in the 1980s represented an intellectual flip-flop from his romantic embrace of the New Left in the 1960s, announced in his 1969 manifesto, *A Theology for Radical Politics*. That book is lush with prorevolution, antiestablishment, anticapitalist, anti–Vietnam War lyrics:

> Corporations are immensely wasteful, the columns of *The Wall Street Journal* give the lie to its editorials. . . . The debts of many decades are coming due: . . . for an economic system based, not on the public good, but on profit; for generations cultivating images of simple manly toughness, violence, and brute mastery over a continent. Brothers and dreamers, there is reason to take heart! . . . A revolution requires long marches, defeats, dry seasons. . . . The revolution is in the human spirit or not at all.[9]

A Theology for Radical Politics is not listed among the titles of nine other Novak books on the frontispiece of *The Spirit of Democratic Capitalism*. What Michael Novak shares with so many other neoconservatives is precisely this spectral shift from the Left to the Right: from socialism to free market entrepreneurialism, from the repudiation of capitalist ideology to the sanctification of it. (Novak offered a brief autobiographical account of that shift in the opening pages of *The Spirit of Democratic Capitalism*. A fuller account is to be found in a chapter from

Gary Dorrien's *The Neoconservative Mind,* "The Renewal of Whiggery: Michael Novak.")[10]

Both *The Spirit of Democratic Capitalism* and *The Catholic Ethic and the Spirit of Capitalism* are dedicated "in homage to Pope John Paul II." The latter work reviews papal encyclicals and other Catholic social teachings from Pope Leo III's 1891 encyclical *Rerum Novarum* to John Paul II's 1991 *Centesimus Annus,* concluding that "the Catholic (and catholic) ethic" provides the best foundation for "democratic capitalism." In paragraph 42 of *Centesimus Annus,* the Pope's affirmation of capitalism "within a strong juridical framework" celebrates "the fundamental and positive role of business, the market, private property and the resulting responsibility for the means of production as well as free human creativity in the economic sector."[11] Novak, Neuhaus, and Weigel have essentially identical appraisals of capitalist ideology and the historic importance of *Centesimus Annus.* Neuhaus's *Doing Well and Doing Good* is a 300-page encomium of that encyclical, or, as the author puts it in his very first sentence, "This is a book . . . about taking care of business and taking care of one another."

Surely, it must be said, business is a legitimate Christian vocation, as legitimate as any other profession insofar as it meets genuine human needs. The hard ethical question is whether the religious promotion of business enterprise combines with political ideas and social policies so as to enhance human well-being or to harm it. It is a burden of this book to assert that prominent political, academic, and theological leaders of the Regressive Revolution have tended to produce more harm than help by their bondage to the Business Mystique—and to Big Money.

Father Neuhaus in the Naked Square

Neuhaus and Novak have shared a spectral shift from the antiestablishment Left of the 1960s to the political and ideological Right of the 1980s and after. In 1970, Neuhaus's radical and romantic counterculturalism was set forth in an essay titled "The Thorough Revolutionary" in which he was at least provisionally willing to support "an armed overthrow of the existing order" or even "revolution for the hell of it."[12] To a greater degree than Novak, Neuhaus has retained the harsh polemical style of his 1960s radicalism and the derisive and vindictive style of the Marxist-Leftist polemics of the 1930s and 1940s.

A transitional tract for Neuhaus was his 1977 monograph (co-authored by sociologist Peter Berger), *To Empower People: The Role of Mediating Structures in Public Policy,* published by the American Enterprise Institute. The "mediating structures" are the social institutions between the individual and the state: family, church, neighborhood, voluntary associations—a concept developed in the 1830s by Alexis de Tocqueville's *Democracy in America* and again in the 1930s and 1940s by the world ecumenical movement, notably by Anglican layman J. H. Oldham. (Some neoconservatives would add business corporations to the list of mediating structures.)

The fundamental issue with "mediating structures" (a.k.a. "intermediate associations" or "civil society") is whether or not their function is invoked to promote genuine republican governance or to promote an ideological antipathy to the public interest and effective government. For Neuhaus, Novak, and other neocons, this concept has increasingly been co-opted for rallying the antigovernment sentiments of the Business Mystique. Meanwhile, Peter Berger, a sometime-Lutheran and longtime-confederate of Neuhaus, received a 1981 grant from the SmithKline Corporation to organize a seminar on Modern Capitalism under the wing of Irving Kristol's Institute for Educational Affairs. That same year, Berger became one of President John Silber's superstar "university professors" at Boston University, where he founded the "eminently pro-capitalist" Institute for the Study of Economic Culture. Berger has explained his alienation from the mainline churches in plain language that doubtless resonates with other neocons less disposed to use it: he "couldn't take the feminist crap" and the "left-liberal-liberationist politics."[13]

Richard Neuhaus became more of a media celebrity with the audacious title of his 1984 book, *The Naked Public Square.*[14] But the thesis of that book turned American political reality on its head with the fanciful claim that religious beliefs and values had been excluded from the conduct of public business. If there is anything that strikes foreign observers of American politics, it is the ubiquity of religiosity throughout our political life.

The messianism and moralism of the Puritan Ethos have been long-lasting: the churches' role in Abolition, Prohibition, and rallying public support for the United Nations; the 1950s' boom times for "piety along the Potomac" and the Christian anticommunism of the Cold War; the 1960s' Christian segregationism versus the Christian civil rights crusade; all sides of the Vietnam War debate; the public controversies ignited by such papal encyclicals as John XXIII's *Pacem in Terris* (1963) and Paul VI's contra-contraception *Humanae Vitae* (1968); the resurgence of a "new Christian Right" in every generation; the assertiveness of the U.S. Catholic Bishops and their pastoral letters on peace and the economy; the Jesse Jackson campaigns; the abortion battles and other culture wars; and, not least, the neoconservative think tanks and their house theologians. All of these lead to one unmistakable conclusion: *There is no naked public square in America.* Our politics are dressed up in religious garb, and always have been.

James Davison Hunter has observed that "the American people have never provided very fertile soil for the growth of purely secular political ideologies. Quite the opposite. America, rather, has always been the 'fertile crescent' of the industrialized world insofar as the development of religious sectarianism is concerned."[15] For Hunter, it is precisely the religious core of political culture that has intensified our culture wars: "The dominant impulse at the present time is toward the polarization of a religiously informed public culture into two relatively distinct moral and ideological camps."[16]

Richard Neuhaus long ago set out to be a cultural warrior and a major force for religious polarization. The persistence and the glee with which he has been crying down doom on mainline Protestantism and the National Council of Churches (NCC), are, at a seemingly more sophisticated level, echoes of what fundamentalists have been crying for years. From some deep well of antipathy, he has compared mainline Protestantism to a dog,

> left to sniff around for crumbs that fell from the tables of the cultural elite. Or, like an aged and somewhat eccentric aunt who shares the house, it was thanked for occasionally helping out with tasks defined and controlled by others. The great white tower of 475 Riverside Drive turned out to be not the capital of the Protestant empire but a marginal service agency trying very hard to be helpful in other people's "progressive causes."[17]

That, we could say, is a bit of a putdown. Moreover, by some arcane arithmetic, Neuhaus calculated that 75 percent of the leaders of mainline Protestantism are either "deeply alienated from the American project" or unwilling or unable to pass his "litmus test" of affirming that American influence is a force for good in the world.[18]

It is a wondrous question why Father Neuhaus keeps up such a predatory and unrelenting assault on churches and councils when he claims they are such pitiable has-beens whom the march of history has long since passed by.

The Institute on Religion and Democracy and the Attack-Mode

Several years before *The Naked Public Square,* Neuhaus had secured a strong Washington connection with the American Enterprise Institute and became a founding father of an aggressive new antimainline institute whose 1981 establishment linked it with the zealots of the first Reagan administration—the Institute on Religion and Democracy (IRD). Other prominent founders of the IRD were Ed Robb, leader of the ultraconservative Good News movement within the United Methodist Church;

Michael Novak; David Jessup and Penn Kemble, 1960s prolabor radicals who had become 1980s conservatives.

It was Richard Neuhaus who authored the IRD's 1981 manifesto titled *Christianity and Democracy,* a document that helped pave the way for the IRD's continuing assaults on the NCC, the World Council of Churches (WCC), and denominational leaders for their positions on peace and social policy issues. The economic ideology of IRD was barely hinted at in a passage acknowledging a "bias in favor of a market economy" in which "the focus is on the production of wealth rather than on the consolidation and redistribution of existing goods."[19] The attack-mode of the IRD was vaguely promised in the manifesto's rebuke of "some leadership circles in the churches" for ignoring or denying "the relationship between Christian faith and democratic governance" and for serving as "apologists for oppression."[20]

The most spectacular of IRD's propaganda triumphs came in January 1983 when the huge-circulation *Reader's Digest* and the CBS television show "60 Minutes" both attacked the NCC and the WCC, with the conspicuous assistance of IRD and Neuhaus. *The Reader's Digest's* "overwrought attack" (according to *Newsweek*) characteristically mixed "innuendo, misleading statements and selective quotes . . . to buttress charges by conservative Christians that ecumenical Protestants may be 'supporting revolution instead of religion' with church tithes."[21] Neuhaus was interviewed by Morley Safer on "60 Minutes" and accused church officials of "telling lies," "consorting" with the killers of Christians, and doing other "evil" things, but Safer did not interview a single one of the accused NCC or denominational staff. The councils were portrayed as pro-Soviet and pro-Castro, proclaiming a gospel according to Karl Marx, not Jesus Christ.

Those 1983 IRD attacks set a pattern of vilification that would continue for more than a dozen years. In her 1993 installation address as IRD president, Diane Knippers reminisced happily about the "60 Minutes" show and Neuhaus's performance thereon as evidence of IRD's success in hastening "the marginalization of wrong-headed influences of the old mainline churches." In a recent interview, Neuhaus gloated that "we pushed that deck of cards and it collapsed."[22]

The political style of the IRD also copied a covert action strategy strangely reminiscent of the communists and the Old Left in the 1930s and 1940s—the concocting of front groups to alienate the affections of constituents from their denominational leaders and budgets. So IRD has spawned Presbyterians for Democracy and Religious Freedom; United Methodist Action for Faith, Freedom, and Family; and Episcopal Action for Faith, Freedom, and Family—all managed from IRD headquarters in Washington; all IRD allies in waging the culture wars.

First Things and
the Great Kulturkampf

Richard John Neuhaus's own zest for the culture wars was evident in the very first issue of a monthly journal called *First Things,* published in 1990 by a new New York–based think tank, the Institute on Religion and Public Life, of which Neuhaus is the founding president. Inaugurating a regular ten-page feature, "The Public Square," at the back of the journal, he wrote that "a new generation of thinkers is coming on line. They know that our society is embroiled in a great *Kulturkampf,* and the war will be won or lost on the terrain of the ideas we take to be most bindingly true. The religio-cultural battle is not the only one, but it is the most critical battle."[23]

Joining Neuhaus's editorial board were Novak, Weigel, and Berger. The launching of that institute and its journal followed almost immediately on Neuhaus's expulsion (in a fight over money) from the directorship of the Center on Religion and Society, a New York outpost of what (after the fight) he termed the "paleoconservative" Rockford Institute. In that same year, he converted from Lutheranism to Roman Catholicism. The next year, he was ordained to the Roman priesthood in a mass celebrated by John Cardinal O'Connor, with William Buckley a participant in the ceremony. Since that conversion, Father Neuhaus has become conspicuously identified with the most traditionalist factions in the Roman Curia, the ultraconservative Opus Dei movement, and the most fervently antiabortion Catholics, as well as with Pope John Paul II's embrace of a "business economy."

The Institute on Religion and Public Life sponsors conferences, colloquia, research fellows, and an annual Erasmus Lecture, with the latter featuring such notable conservatives as Joseph Cardinal Ratzinger, Wolfhart Pannenberg, and Midge Decter. Both the programs and publications of the Institute have presented at least an appearance of some ideological diversity and dialogue. But Neuhaus's monthly "Public Square" columns in *First Things* have continued a relentless fusillade against the innumerable persons and institutions on his enemies list:

> *The New York Times* ("the sleazy old lady of American journalism," "crassly partisan in an essentially frivolous way")
> *The New Yorker* ("specious, spurious, meretricious, and dishonest")
> *The Nation* ("the storm-tossed flagscow of the left")
> CBS/TV ("leading the way in the indulgence of religious bigotry")
> Bill Moyers ("an insufferable prig")

The National Catholic Reporter ("the floundering flagscow of the Catholic left")

Commonweal ("paleoliberal")

The Christian Century ("a declining referent")

Christianity and Crisis ("betrayed a noble tradition" and "died of a terminal lack of interest")

The World Council of Churches (In December 1992, Neuhaus wrote: "World history and the vibrant centers of world Christianity have moved on, leaving the WCC to drift in the fetid backwaters of the politicized religion produced by eviscerated faith and discredited ideology.")

The National Council of Churches ("that marginal service agency," part of "that crazy band to keep beating the drums to make other people sacrifice")

The Protestant "old-line" or "sideline" (especially the Episcopal, Methodist, and Presbyterian churches)

The National Conference of Catholic Bishops (especially Archbishop Rembert Weakland of Milwaukee, who directed the 1986 pastoral letter *Economic Justice for All,* for being a "star in the tired theater of Catholic delinquency")

Dissenting Catholic theologians (Richard McBrien, Richard McCormick, Charles Curran, Hans Küng)

Liberation theology and Third World theologians

Feminist theologians (Rosemary Ruether, Elisabeth Schüssler Fiorenza, Carter Heyward)

Pro-Choice groups (Planned Parenthood, Catholics for a Free Choice, Religious Coalition for Reproductive Choice)

Gay and lesbian rights groups

The American Civil Liberties Union and other church-state separationists

"Civil rights leaders, as they used to be called," who support affirmative action

Bill Clinton, Jimmy Carter, George McGovern, Ted Kennedy, Mario Cuomo, Justice Harry Blackmun, George Kennan

The sheer vitriol of many of these attacks alternates with gentler, wittier, more patronizing putdowns. What is all too rare in "The Public Square" is evidence of civility and a genuinely dialogical spirit. Just how much investment the corporate foundations sustaining *First Things* have in all these personal invectives is difficult to determine.

Richard Neuhaus and Michael Novak have also served to associate neoconservative theologians and their think tanks with the Christian Coalition, whose convention they have addressed. "I think it is vitally important," says

Neuhaus, "that this vibrant resurgence of political activism in American life be brought into ecumenical conversation with other Christians."[24]

Ethics for Corporate Warfare

The EPPC was founded in 1976 as an autonomous adjunct to George-town University, but was separated from the university in 1980, at least partly in response to faculty doubts about its academic integrity. The Center's founder, Ernest W. Lefever, is another case study of the swing from Left to Right. Originally a Church of the Brethren pacifist who traveled widely for the Fellowship of Reconciliation, he worked briefly for the NCC's international department in the 1950s and later became an aide to Senator Hubert Humphrey. However, during his years as a research scholar at the Brookings Institution and the Institute for Defense Analyses, he became an ardent Cold Warrior and aggressive defender of U.S. military policies in Vietnam. His developing conservative, promilitary identity attracted the notice of corporations with prime defense contracts—corporations whose financial aid would soon benefit the new center that he organized.

Lefever's brief moment of national fame came when the U.S. Senate overwhelmingly rejected his 1981 nomination by President Reagan to serve as Assistant Secretary of State for Human Rights and Humanitarian Affairs. That rejection came after sixty organizations (including the National Council of Churches, the American Friends Service Committee, and the Union of American Hebrew Congregations) had combined to form an Ad Hoc Committee of the Human Rights Community to oppose the nomination. Their opposition was based largely on Lefever's own opposition to human rights standards for diplomatic business with "friendly states," while he advocated such standards toward "adversary states" like the Soviet Union. He regarded the pro-apartheid government of South Africa as such a "friendly state" and an ally against the Soviet Union. Lefever charged that the anticolonial and pro-human rights policies of the Carter administration had given "aid and comfort to the Marxists." He had made numerous trips to South Africa and was opposed to the churches' campaign for corporate disinvestment as a strategy to overcome apartheid. He also opposed the churches' boycott of the Nestlé Company's products in the controversy over that company's exports of infant formula to poor countries. Media revelations of Nestlé's financial support of Lefever's center helped to defeat the nomination.

Shortly after that defeat, Lefever told this writer that all the national publicity around the Senate hearings had been a boon to the EPPC because it had attracted substantial new sources of funding from corporations and foundations. A further "consolation" came the next year

(1982–1983) when the U.S. Information Agency granted Lefever's center nearly $200,000 to promote the views of pro-Reagan administration scholars and journalists resisting the antinuclear peace movements in Europe.

Lefever's most substantial attacks on the churches and the ecumenical movement came in two volumes purporting to trace the ideological captivity of the WCC to Marxism and to pro-Soviet and pro-Castro policies. In 1979, *Amsterdam to Nairobi: The World Council of Churches and the Third World* (with foreword by George Will) was summarized in the center's flier:

> On the long road from the Amsterdam Assembly (1948) to the Nairobi Assembly (1975) and to the present, the WCC has moved from a largely democratic concept of political responsibility to a more radical ideology that by 1975 embraced the concept and practice of "liberation theology."
> . . . This "revolutionary" theology has much in common with current Marxist concepts. The WCC position on some issues has been indistinguishable from that taken in Moscow or Havana.[25]

Particularly objectionable to Lefever were the WCC's Programme to Combat Racism and its humanitarian grants to African liberation movements; the WCC's criticisms of transnational corporations and of U.S. policy in Vietnam; and its "reluctance to criticize gross violations of human rights in Communist countries." Ethicist Roger Shinn, both a WCC veteran and an original member of Lefever's Board of Advisers, regarded the book as "badly researched and poorly written" and had actually resigned from the EPPC board earlier because he found that board to be too heavily tilted to the Right.[26]

Lefever's sequel, *Nairobi to Vancouver: The World Council of Churches and the World, 1975–87,* offered a similar polemic against the "radicalism" of both the WCC and the NCC, while preaching the moral virtues of capitalism. The WCC, he charged,

> is influential in perverse ways, primarily as a continuing source of confusion and as an active supporter of revolutionary elites, both religious and secular. Many WCC leaders . . . are active in a global network of radical academics, scientists, journalists, and politicians that provides ideas, training, and money for "liberation" efforts driven by Marxist-Leninist fervor and frequently supported by the Soviet Union. . . . The ecumenical movement as manifest in the WCC and the U.S. National Council of Churches . . . has failed in its culture-forming mission in the Western world [and its] social witness has become obsolescent, marginal, irrelevant, or worse.[27]

In numerous details as well as broad generalizations and caricatures, that volume exhibited careless scholarship and venomous language.

Under Lefever's direction, the EPPC also developed study projects on public education (to show that social science texts were failing to transmit "core Western values"), the mass media (alleging political biases in network television), and "the ideological assault on the corporation and the competitive market" by the churches.

Lefever retired from the EPPC presidency in 1989 and was succeeded by George Weigel, the youngest of the Catholic neoconservative think-tank triumvirate. Weigel serves on the boards of both the Institute on Religion and Democracy and Neuhaus's Institute on Religion and Public Life, frequently contributing articles to Neuhaus's *First Things*. But Weigel seems committed to a more irenic and civil discourse across a somewhat wider ideological spectrum than Neuhaus or IRD or Lefever has tolerated. He has also significantly extended the range of religious and cultural issues featured by the EPPC as well as the media outreach of his center. Weigel's ten books include *Tranquillitas Ordinis: The Present Failure and Future Promise of American Catholic Thought on War and Peace* and *Soul of the World: Notes on the Future of Public Catholicism,* the latter with particular attention to the economic and social teachings of Pope John Paul II.

In 1996, Weigel yielded the presidency of the EPPC to Elliott Abrams, the former Reagan administration official implicated in the Iran-Contra affair. Weigel continues in a leadership role at EPPC as a senior scholar.

Funding and Defunding

Beneath all questions that have been raised about the motivations, scholarly merit, and Christian fidelity of these religiously oriented think tanks are the institutional realities: these think tanks are not grounded in the churches but in the world of corporate business and foundation largesse. That in itself is hardly cause for criticism, but in these cases the correspondence between their faith-claimed theology and the self-interests of their prime funders is absolutely clear.

Leon Howell, former editor of *Christianity and Crisis,* recently completed a thorough investigation of think-tank finances, the purpose of which was to uncover "some of the ways in which funds from foundations largely unknown to the public have fueled the war of ideas. And it is to help us understand that the consistent ideological attacks on the mainline churches are part of a larger strategy of assaulting institutions in the arts, education, labor and media as well as targeting such social issues as abortion and gay rights."[28]

Howell's report, *Funding the War of Ideas,* focused on the four conservative foundations most active in funding (and concerting their funding) of right-wing think tanks. The four are the Bradley, Olin, Scaife, and

Smith-Richardson foundations. Known as the "four sisters," these corporate siblings provided grants of $57 million in 1993 to such entities as the American Enterprise Institute, the Heritage Foundation, the Manhattan Institute, National Empowerment Television (featuring Newt Gingrich and the National Rifle Association), the Madison Center for Educational Affairs (sponsor of seventy conservative papers on sixty-six college campuses), and Emmett Tyrell's inflammatory journal, *The American Spectator.*[29]

More pertinent to this chapter and to the religion-targeted institutes are the "four sisters" grants that provided the lion's share of budget support for the Institute on Religion and Democracy, the Institute on Religion and Public Life, and the Ethics and Public Policy Center. In 1993, for example:

> The IRD received $260,000 of its total revenue of $483,000 from three of the "four sisters," with most of the balance from other foundations. In IRD's two critical start-up years, the "sisters" had provided 89 percent of its income.
>
> Neuhaus's Institute on Religion and Public Life received $896,000 in grants ($690,000 of that from the "sisters") out of $1.2 million in total income.
>
> The EPPC received $1 million in grants (including $670,000 from the "sisters") out of a total income of $1.1 million. In the EPPC's early years, prime military contractors were major supporters.[30]

These may seem like modest amounts in the world of foundation grants and corporate finance. But in the war of ideas, especially at a time of growing fiscal stress for denominational and ecumenical bodies, such targeted grants to media-savvy ideologues can create a one-sided struggle—and have done so in recent years. In another sense, there are indeed two sides in this struggle. One side consists of these substantial strategic grants. The other is the right-wing strategy, funded by these grants, to *defund* national church bodies by provoking the alienation of their constituencies. In the total reckoning, the *defunding* may matter much more than the *funding*.

8

WHAT DOES A
GOOD IDEOLOGY REQUIRE?

The claim that redemption in Christ has a social dimension . . . is still under continuous challenge by conservative Christians who seek to invalidate any theology . . . that would make socioeconomic liberation an intrinsic part of the meaning of redemption.
—Rosemary Radford Ruether,
Sexism and God-Talk

Ideology is the picture of how society should be and how such a society is justified. It is an interconnected set of ideas and beliefs that articulates how the basic values of a group of people apply to the distribution of power in society. An ideology is the vision that gives a cohesive shape to social values and the dream of how the social order is to be organized by those values. . . . Part of the stagnation of the American governmental system at [the] end of the twentieth century is the paling of ideology. People lack a compelling vision of what society should be and hopes of what it could be.
—Stephen Charles Mott,
A Christian Perspective on Political Thought

If indeed ideology is both inevitable and imperative, with a potential for human good and social transformation, what must a "good" ideology be and do? Given ideology's functions as a set of beliefs and symbols that serve to interpret social reality and to motivate political action, what are the necessary components of a constructive ideology for Christians? Left or Right or Centrist, liberal or conservative, capitalist or socialist, pacifist or nonpacifist, what makes for a mature and faithful ideology?

A half century ago, after the totalitarian ideologies of Fascism and National Socialism had been overwhelmed in war, only to be followed by a Cold War in which capitalism and communism escalated their mutual hostility, sociologist Joseph Roucek offered a graphic picture of the requirements of an effective ideology:

> its completeness and internal coherence
> its gorgeous vision of the future
> its ability to hold men's imaginations
> its pretense to provide a universal frame of reference of good
> and evil

its consistency
its convincing criticism of the present and picture of the future
and its ability to circumvent countercriticism[1]

Both the power and the perils of ideology are suggested in that description.

This brief chapter will not pretend to offer a complete response to the question of a mature ideology. It offers only a provisional agenda for theological and ethical reflection—a checklist of at least some of the topics that must be addressed by an ideology that aspires to be both faithful and empowering.

1. God's Action in History

Christians proclaim God as Creator, as the Alpha and Omega of all history. How does the Creation reflect the love and the power of God? Is there a moral law written into the Creation? If so, how may we know it? And what is it? In the dramas of history, does "the arc of the universe bend toward justice," as Martin Luther King, Jr. believed?

How does God continue to act in history? Is God's action political in any sense? Does God take sides in human conflicts? If so, whose side? The rich? The poor? The powerful? The weak? Or all of the above?

Does God "intervene" to prevent suffering? If so, why hasn't God intervened to prevent slavery, or war, or the Holocaust, or atomic bombs, or AIDS, or the deaths of thousands of children every day due to poverty, malnutrition, and disease?

What is the balance between God's action and human action? How real and how radical are human freedom and responsibility in the shaping of history? Would God permit the human race to annihilate itself? Why, or why not?

What is the end of history, in the purposes and providence of God?

2. A Moral Anthropology

Christians proclaim that all persons are created in the image of God. How are we to view the moral and social capacities of human nature in the light of that image—but also in view of the universal empirical evidence of human sinfulness, both personal and corporate? How will we balance the marvelous record of human creativity, courage, and sacrifice with the appalling record of human violence, treachery, and greed?

Is human nature fundamentally aggressive and competitive? Or is it fundamentally sociable and cooperative? How should a political vision of the future take account of either view?

Is there a Christian basis for proclaiming human rights? If so, what are the most basic human rights? How do those rights relate to human responsibilities?

What is the human capacity for social change, for the transformation of basic social institutions? Is genuine progress possible, impossible, or inevitable? Is human nature so depraved that a "realistic" moral anthropology must serve more or less as a justification for the status quo? What is the right balance between optimism and pessimism in assessing the political potential of human nature?

What is the relationship between personal conversion and social transformation? Must one precede the other? If so, which comes first, and why? Is salvation social as well as personal?

3. Basic Social Institutions

Christians since biblical times have proclaimed beliefs about the family, government, and the economy. A critical task for a faithful ideology is to interpret the relationship of such social institutions to the purposes and will of God, to each other, and to society as a whole.

Is the family an institution grounded in God's good creation? If so, what is normative for family relationships? What rights and responsibilities belong to the family? What is the responsibility of government for the well-being of the family, especially of children?

Is government an institution grounded in God's good creation? Are human beings created as political animals, to govern and be governed, to exercise power and to struggle for common purposes? Or is government an institution that developed only as a consequence of human sinfulness, perhaps as a divinely appointed remedy for depravity? Or should governments be abolished altogether in favor of maximum human freedom? How should Christians maintain a balance between positive and negative view of government and politics?

Is economic life grounded in God's good creation? Are human beings made for work and to struggle for physical survival, wealth, and/or abundance? Should work be basically competitive or cooperative?

What are the ethical foundations of political economy? What is the proper role of government in relation to economic institutions: separation, promotion, regulation, control, or ownership? What is the right balance between private and public claims to property? How are governmental and economic institutions to act in behalf of human rights?

What other institutions, if any, are grounded in God's good creation? Health? Education? The arts? Communications? Religion?

4. The World of Nations

Christians and Jews share scriptures that portray nations as prime actors in relation to God and one another. The testimony of biblical times is that nations are called to justice and peace, but they are often idolatrous and iniquitous. They rise and they fall under the judgment of God. But there is also the vision of the day when all the nations—from all tribes and peoples and tongues, especially those who have suffered great tribulation—will come together before the Lord God and will no longer suffer hunger or thirst or hurt or sorrow.

A faithful ideology will ask: What is the special place of nations in the purposes of God and in the whole human family? Is there a unique vocation for any particular nation, given its history and heritage and culture? What is the role of prophecy in celebrating and safeguarding the nationhood of a particular people or in leading a people to repentance for past sins and inhumanities?

Is the sovereign nation-state a permanent political system or only a provisional entity that may evolve into some other form of governance?

How should the structures and policies of government and economy within the nation be shaped by the interests of other nations, intergovernmental structures, the world economy, and global ecology? Are ideologies for "society" or "the economy" adequate if they do not articulate their ideas within the context of international systems? What is the place of such concepts as world community, interdependence, common security, the international common good, and global governance in a faithful ideology?

5. The Moral Burdens of History

Christian faith takes history seriously as the arena not only of God's active purposes but also of the human struggle for justice and peace.

A faithful ideology will seek to understand the moral burdens of history: to interpret political, social, and economic history in morally significant terms, with particular attention to the victims of violence, poverty, and oppression—and to past actions that vitally affect the well-being of the whole society or the whole human family. It will seek and hear the stories, the faith perspectives, and the narratives of moral struggle of marginalized peoples from "the underside of history," as well as of those in privileged positions of power and leadership. It will know how to analyze the realities of power and its uses and abuses so as to demythologize self-aggrandizing histories, whether in textbooks, official rhetoric, or public policy debate, being especially alert to the fabrication of myths and data by national and economic interests.

How may the injustices of the past be rectified by present institutions and policies? What restitution or reparations, if any, are in order? What "affirmative actions" may be necessary for the sake of genuine equality of opportunity? What transformations of power structures are required if justice is to be done?

In confronting present or potential conflicts between nations or groups, to what extent is acknowledgment of past wrongs a moral and political prerequisite of conflict resolution? Is repentance a precondition of reconciliation in most political conflicts? Are nations capable of repentance and forgiveness?

What does each generation owe to past generations? To future generations?

A faithful ideology will devote special attention to these issues of intergenerational ethics.

6. Violence and Nonviolence

Christians remain deeply divided over the ethical issues of violence: military force, deterrence, police powers, revolution, social change, penal justice, capital punishment. A faithful ideology cannot ignore these issues. It will inquire into the legitimacy and limits of political violence, whether by governments, intergovernmental institutions, or nongovernmental groups. It will ask the following:

1. When, if ever, is organized violence morally justifiable as an act of justice or social transformation, or perhaps as the lesser of evils? Does the ideology celebrate or romanticize violence as part of its political appeal?

2. Does the ideology accept the initial presumption of nonviolence that is the shared commitment of both pacifism and just-war theory, the latter justifying a decision for war only as a last resort (after satisfying the criteria of just cause, just intent, legitimate authority, and reasonable hope of success)?

3. Does the ideology take account of the realities of systemic violence in political, economic, and social structures? How does it interpret the relationship of unjust structures to the demand for order and to the tasks of reconciliation and peacemaking?

4. Is the ideology open to every possibility of the creative and transforming potential of nonviolence? Does it have a conception of how to overcome violence and create a culture of peace?

7. A Vision of the Future

Christian faith is a "theology of hope"—a conviction that conversion is possible, that persons and societies and the whole world may be redeemed, that the cruelest burdens of history may at last be overcome.

A faithful ideology will set forth a vision of a society and a world that promises a more just, peaceable, and humane life for all people. Such a vision will be expressed in beliefs and symbols that empower its advocates with a significant political identity and inspire their imagination and commitment.

1. What kind of society do we really want for our own future and for our children and future generations?

2. What kind of government and political life will contribute most to the realization of such a vision?

3. What patterns of economic life and power will help most to overcome the massive poverty, gross inequalities, and exploitative relationships in the U.S. and world economy?

4. What changes in our culture, education, and religious life would be auspicious for such a transformation?

5. Dare we really dream that this world does not have to be this way forever?

6. What human hopes, if any, must be deferred to the end of history?

8. A Political Ecclesiology

Ecclesiology originally referred to study of the art and architecture of the church but has acquired a much broader meaning—study of ideas and doctrines about the church as an institution. It is theology about the church itself.

Political ecclesiology, a term of recent development, concerns ideas and doctrines about the mission of the church in the world of nations, governments, and politics. A faithful ideology will ask the following:

1. How should the gospel of Jesus Christ define the political responsibilities of the church?

2. How should law define the relationship between church and state: establishment, separation, cooperation, or conflict?

3. How do the church's universal mission and transnational institutions shape the church's ideas about relationships with any state and the multiplicity of nation-states?

4. Should the church serve primarily as the model of an alternative community or as an active participant in public policy?

5. Should the church's public witness be limited to the individual vocations of its members, or should the corporate church also seek to influence politics? If the latter, how should this be done?

6. Should the worship and educational life of the church be open to political controversy, or should the church seek to transcend or avoid such controversy?

7. Should the church or its leaders ever identify with a political party, or avoid all partisan identification? Should the church or its leaders ever identify with a particular economic or social group or institution?

8. If the church avoids speaking on political issues, does it thereby risk sanctifying the status quo and its injustices?

9. How should the church's public witness take account of the diversity of denominations and world religions?

10. Finally, what role should the church play in confronting and/or nurturing ideologies?

The questions raised in this chapter will be very partially addressed in the two concluding chapters. Taken together, they may persuade the reader that ideology is a huge subject, inseparable from the most foundational religious and philosophical beliefs, the whole range of human institutions, and the basic methodologies and perennial topics of ethics. Indeed it is all that. But these questions may also persuade the reader that the demands of this subject far exceed the supply of knowledge and wisdom of this writer. That is also true.

9

DEMOCRATIC HUMANISM: TOWARD A CONVIVIAL WORLD

> The most powerful ideologies of our age all suffer from having acquired their shape and substance in the 18th and 19th centuries, or very much earlier, before the world in which we live had come fully into view. They are like medieval maps of the world, charming but dangerous for navigating unfamiliar seas.
>
> —Robert A. Dahl,
> *Dilemmas of Pluralist Democracy*

> What we lack and what we desperately need is a new ideology, not of the fanatical, closed-system character . . . but most certainly a broad, plastic ideology . . . which will enable us to transcend our current stagnation.
>
> —Chaim Waxman,
> *The End of Ideology Debate*

The purpose of this book is to encourage the renewal of ideology in America—for the sake of "a more perfect union" and an Earth that "shall be fair, and all her people one." Our definition presupposes that ideology comprehends more than economic issues, for such issues must be set in the context of social reality and political responsibility. The pernicious subordination of politics to economics, or even the baleful effort to maintain economic ideas in disregard of political philosophy altogether, is the source of ethical impotence and the vitiation of democracy. As political columnist Mark Shields puts it: "Capitalism has shown itself to be a dynamic economic theory. But it is neither a coherent social policy nor political philosophy."[1] Both capitalist and socialist ideologies have tended to devalue the primacy of government as the institution rightly authorized to speak and act for society as a whole.

The central importance of ideology for a society's political vitality is underscored by Lester Thurow's recent volume, *The Future of Capitalism:* "Successful societies have to unite around a powerful story with a sustaining ideology. If there is no story to tell, leaders have no agenda—and no self-confidence in what they are doing."[2] Thurow sees American society as increasingly rent by social and economic inequalities and stumbling toward stagnation without a compelling vision of its long-range future. American politics now offers "debates between parties on the right who want to go back to a mythical past" and parties on the left devoid of any clear agendas:

> What does democracy mean when political parties don't have different ideological beliefs—different visions of the nature of the system and of where the promised land lies—so that they can debate alternative roads into the future? Elections become popularity polls swirling around trivial issues and dependent upon who looks best on television. . . . To work, democracy needs a vision of utopia—a route to a better society—a vision of what it is that transcends narrow sectarian self-interest.[3]

Lester Thurow assumes the endurance of capitalism as the only ideological option for America, but wants to improve its vision and fortify its commitments.

This chapter assumes a rather different task. It rejects both capitalism and socialism as inadequate ideologies for the American and world future—partly because they have too many faults in common. This chapter proposes an alternative vision—*democratic humanism.*

Democratic capitalism is proving again and again to be an oxymoron symbolized by reducing *democratic* to a feeble adjective for an economic system that is corrupting and devitalizing the integrity of democratic institutions.

Democratic socialism is severely hampered by its very vocabulary, its multiplicity of competing definitions, its record of weakness in the United States, and its unfortunate if unfair association with the recent collapse of Marxist-Leninist socialism in Eastern Europe. Nearly a century ago, sociologist Werner Sombart declared that in the United States "all the socialist utopias have foundered upon roast beef and apple pie"—by which he referred to the seemingly unlimited wealth and opportunity of this country.[4] Sombart told only a half-truth, for a modest fellowship of democratic socialists has endured through the generations precisely because of the perversity of imperious wealth and unequal opportunity. Moreover, socialists first conceived many of the social policy innovations of America's incomplete welfare state.

Democratic humanism, as we will presently elaborate, presupposes the primacy of politics over economics and a human rights–based society prior to and sovereign over any economic system.

Market Fundamentalism

The case for capitalist triumphalism since the end of the Cold War, especially the lyrics of "market fundamentalism" broadcast to Central and Eastern Europe and heralding "the end of history," has become less and less credible in the face of the social chaos and acute suffering in that "postsocialist" region now experiencing a resurgence of communists and other authoritarians. A report from the United Nations Children's Fund (UNICEF) has found that the "unsettling years of transition from Communism to free-market democracies have left the most vulnerable people of Eastern and Central Europe significantly poorer, less healthy . . . and more prone to accidental death and suicide." The report concluded that economic changes have "provoked a deterioration of unparalleled proportions in human welfare throughout most of the region." The rising incidence of disease, stress, malnutrition, and alcoholism is producing a "health crisis" that is eroding public support for market reforms.[5]

The triumphalist case is further discredited by the spreading swamp of indulgences and injustices in most consumption-driven Western societies. And it is debased by the abject poverty and misery of most countries in the world's South, compounded by deepening debt, the harsh market measures of the International Monetary Fund and other institutions of global capitalism, and the incapacity and/or unwillingness of the United States and other Northern nations to help by agreeing to major changes in trade, aid, and monetary policies.

At the very end of R. H. Tawney's 1922 masterpiece, *Religion and the Rise of Capitalism,* there is a passage that, alas, speaks all too appropriately to our present ideological predicament and the licentious greed and materialism it camouflages. Modern capitalism, wrote Tawney,

> is that whole system of appetites and values, with its deification of the life of snatching to hoard, and hoarding to snatch, which now, in the hour of its triumph, while the plaudits of the crowd still ring in the ears of the gladiators and the laurels are still unfaded on their brows, seems sometimes to leave a taste as of ashes on the lips of a civilization which has brought to the conquest of its material environment resources unknown in earlier ages, but which has not yet learned to master itself.[6]

A huge difficulty with market fundamentalism is that it obscures the empirical realities of political and economic power structures. In every society that claims a free market, there are severe constraints—not just government enterprises, protections, and regulations, but also monopolies, conglomerates, and collusive practices that seek to dominate the market.

The market as such does not reflect true demand in terms of human needs. The world is full of demanding, agonizing, unmet human needs; the demand to which the market responds is only in terms of purchasing power, which the poorest people do not possess. People without the power to buy are excluded from the market.

Market prices do not necessarily reflect the true costs or values of goods. True costs may include such externalities of production as pollution, resource depletion, and impaired health of workers, which the tax-paying public may or may not agree to assume. Prices may be set artificially high by monopolies, or below costs in order to undercut less powerful competitors.

The market makes no provision for equality among producers. Historically, American farmers and agrarian Third World countries have sought government intervention to secure parity vis-à-vis industrial and financial institutions and nations. Although various U.S. farm blocs succeeded politically in winning government price supports, even as farming largely evolved into corporate agribusiness, the United States and other predominantly capitalist powers have yet to vindicate the principle of parity in world trade for most Third World producers of primary products.

The market makes no provision for equality of access to economic information, nor any guarantee of truthful information about products on the market. It does not protect consumer interests and welfare unless compelled to do so by government regulations.

While the market promotes private affluence for many persons, it typically fails to generate adequate resources to meet either public sector needs or the special needs of lower income persons and communities. As long ago as 1958, John Kenneth Galbraith's *The Affluent Society* colorfully described this contradiction between private affluence and public squalor:

> The family which takes its mauve and cerise, air-conditioned, power-steered and power-braked automobile out for a tour passes through cities that are badly paved, made hideous by litter, blighted buildings, billboards and posts for wires that should long since have been put underground. They pass on into a countryside that has been rendered invisible by commercial art. . . . Is this, indeed, the American genius?[7]

To be sure, the market provides stimuli to initiative, invention, and productivity. It provides society with a mechanism of exchange. But the market as such is not a full-fledged social philosophy, much less a humane social ethic. Karl Polanyi wrote that the acceptance of a self-regulating market risks the subordination of society itself to supposed economic laws:

> To allow the market mechanism to be the sole director of the fate of human beings and their natural environment, indeed, even of the amount and use of purchasing power, would result in the demolition of society. . . . Robbed of the protective covering of cultural institutions, human beings would perish from the effects of social exposure; they would die as the victims of acute social dislocation through vice, perversion, crime, and starvation.[8]

That, in tragic fact, is the recurring fate of numberless Americans and Eastern Europeans in our time. Echoing Polanyi in a theological critique, metaphorically titled *God the Economist*, M. Douglas Meeks rebuked the idolatry of market logic for its commodification of human relationships and its exclusion of God from market discourse.[9]

In another essay, Polanyi noted that it was not Marxism that invented economic determinism. It was faith in the "free market" that "created the delusion of economic determinism as a general law for all human society. . . . Instead of the economic system being embedded in social relationships, these relationships were now embedded in the economic system."[10]

It has remained beyond the imagination of most of us, most of the time, to recognize that societies professing to be capitalist and regimes professing to be communist have shared many of the common failings of Western industrialization. They have idolized technology at the expense of community, devastated the environment, militarized their economies and their governments, and alienated their workers. A quarter century ago, Michael Harrington noted both the commonality and the variations:

> Under capitalism, an intricate system of antagonistic cooperation makes a single individual more productive than a thousand once were. Science . . . is casually employed for private purposes with revolutionary public consequences. This creates the highest living standard ever known, rots the great cities, befouls the air and water, and embitters classes, generations, and races. Under Communism, these contradictions are collectivized, not resolved. The state owns the means of production, and a bureaucratic elite owns the state. Its interests, which are every bit as egotistic as the corporation, are imposed upon the system by totalitarian command. The antisocial is thus consciously planned rather than being dictated by the "will" of the market.[11]

Given the current drive toward market fundamentalism, Christians are called to the task of demythologizing as a theological imperative. The real issue is not market or no market. It is the question: market within what pattern of social vision, political power, and responsibility? And within what theologically grounded view of human nature? E. J. Dionne, Jr., acknowledges that "the new conservatism is not wrong in defending the economic market in its proper sphere. It *is* wrong in trying to apply a market model to almost all aspects of human life."[12]

Capitalism versus Democracy

A fundamental ideological question for our time is the compatibility or incompatibility of capitalism with democracy. American society has become more democratic only insofar as it has authorized government to curb the dehumanizing drives of prodigal capitalism—which is to say, only insofar as it has become something other than a strictly capitalist society. A truly democratic society will never forfeit all its civil institutions to the private powers of profit and wealth.

In a fiftieth anniversary retrospective on Joseph Schumpeter's 1942 classic, *Capitalism, Socialism, and Democracy,* political scientist Ralph Miliband declared "capitalist democracy" to be

> a contradiction in terms, for it encapsulates two opposed systems. On the one hand there is capitalism, a system . . . that demands the existence of a relatively small class of people who own and control the main means of industrial, commercial, and financial activity, as well as a major part of the means of communication; these people thereby exercise a totally disproportionate amount of influence on politics and society both in their own countries and in lands far beyond their own borders. On the other hand there is democracy, which is based on the *denial* of such preponderance, and which requires a rough *equality of condition* that capitalism . . . repudiates by its very nature.[13]

This conviction that democracy and capitalism are contradictory and mutually exclusive ideologies must be qualified by the recognition that there are no societies in which either ideology is incarnated in pristine and purest form. The reality is that there are many societies (including the United States) in which an incomplete democracy coexists and struggles with a somewhat inhibited capitalism in an unsettled state of ideological schizophrenia. In that extremely qualified sense, then, democracy and capitalism are not necessarily mutually exclusive. But the efforts of some conservative and neoconservative apologists for capitalism (such as Novak, Neuhaus, Berger, and Weigel) to proclaim a coherent unity of "democratic capitalism" defy credibility in the face of history and current trends.

The failure of capitalism, American-style, to match political democracy with economic democracy—or, rather, to authenticate political democracy with economic democracy—is exposed not only in the severe inequalities of political and economic power: it is manifest in the growing and glaring inequalities of income and wealth. In the past quarter century, class consciousness has intensified as millions of middle-class Americans have felt excluded from economic growth and the prosperity of their upper-income compatriots, while tens of millions of poor people have been persistently humiliated by what Thurow calls the "revival of survival-of-the-fittest capitalism."

The evidence of escalating economic and social inequalities is stark. From 1973 to 1995, the real per capita gross domestic product (GDP) rose 36 percent, while the hourly wages of (nonsupervisory) workers actually *declined* 14 percent. In the decade of the 1980s, 64 percent of earnings gains and 90 percent of income gains went to the top 1 percent of the American population.[14] Personally dramatizing this rapidly widening gap are the CEOs of major corporations whose average income (after taxes) amounted to 12 times that of factory workers in 1960; rose to 35 times in 1974 and 135 times by 1995—while the real income of male workers with high school diplomas dropped by 30 percent between 1973 and 1993.[15]

The robber barons are back, and the nation is regressing to a severe neostratification.

The Seven Deadly D's

This growing ideological strain between "the egalitarian foundations of democracy and the inegalitarian reality of capitalism"[16] has contributed greatly to the breakdown of political infrastructure in America. That breakdown can be analyzed in terms of "seven deadly D's": (1) the *derangement* of the nominating processes through costly, debilitating, and unrepresentative primary elections intended to be "progressive"; (2) the *decline* of political parties in terms of both membership and ideology; (3) *divided* government without clear party accountability between the presidency and Congress; (4) the *disarray* of Congress itself; (5) the *demoralization* of the bureaucracy; (6) the *devolution* of political authority in matters of economic and social responsibility; and (7) the *displacement* of the powers of governance by private aggregates of special interests.[17]

The Regressive Revolution clearly has vested interests in abetting this political breakdown and displacing the very powers of governance. Neocapitalist Social Darwinism seeks licentious freedom from government control even as it seeks to control government itself. Its influence is exercised by great private aggregates of economic power—parapolitical structures that Christians would do well to regard as the "principalities and powers" with which they must wrestle if the public interest and the general welfare are to be served. These aggregates tend to coalesce into imperious "complexes": a multi-industrial complex (as in a tobacco company in the food business or a steel corporation using its tax breaks to buy an oil company); a military-industrial complex (actually much more complex in its institutional entanglements or, as the United Methodist Bishops' 1986 pastoral letter, *In Defense of Creation,* put it, the "military-industrial-political-scientific-educational-recreational-media-religious complex"); a medical-industrial complex (now costing $1 trillion a year); a media-industrial complex (advertisers who propagate consumerism, shape entertainment, and view the news as show business); a highway-industrial complex (partial to autos, gasoline, and suburbs at the expense of rails, mass transit, and cities); a development-industrial complex (builders, banks, Savings and Loans, and suburban malls that conspire to ravage the environment and impoverish urban neighborhoods). In shorthand, these parapolitical structures may be referred to as four MICs, a HIC, and a DIC.

These conglomerates of economic power have captured political power by waging ideological warfare against the welfare state. That warfare has been waged not only by direct financing of campaigns but through those pretentious "think tanks" that have seized the initiative across the entire agenda of public policy.

The Inevitably Mixed Economy

Every modern industrial society, whatever its ideological pretensions, in fact operates a mixed economy. However, the particular mix of public and private sector enterprises and controls varies greatly from country to country. The mix is rarely if ever defined simply by ideology; it is determined at least in part by political bargaining and by the pragmatic accommodation of economic and other interests. Yale political theorist Robert A. Dahl, in an essay explaining "Why Free Markets Are Not Enough," observed that "every democratic country has rejected the practice, if not always the ideology, of unregulated competitive markets. . . . In every democratic country the market economy is modified by government intervention."[18]

The historic record of government intervention in the American economy is so substantial in ventures that could well be regarded as "socialist" (and sometimes is) that the "capitalist" label for the economy is exposed as exceedingly inadequate. The list of such ventures includes both early and modern toll roads, the Erie Canal, public schools, free land under the Homestead Act, land grant colleges, railroads west of the Mississippi, early airline subsidies through the postal service, public airports, public housing, Social Security, Medicare, the G.I. Bill for higher education, the interstate highway system, municipal power companies, municipal transit systems, the Tennessee Valley Authority, atomic energy, biotechnology, space exploration. Several of these ventures have escaped the "socialist" label by virtue of the protective coloration provided by their identification with "national defense": the interstate highways were instituted by the National Defense Highways Act; university scholarships were rationalized by the National Defense Education Act; moon flights were a product of the space race with the Russians; the Internet began as a project for a bombproof military communication system.[19]

Beyond these special investments in "defense" needs is the larger, continuing reality of "military socialism"—that vast sector of corporate life composed of interlocking directorates between the Pentagon and "private" military contractors, largely closed to competitive bidding and public scrutiny, heavily subsidized as a special kind of "welfare state," served by thousands of retired military officers recycled as industrial executives, and sustained by military budgets which, in some years, have been larger than the after-tax profits of all other private corporations.

Thurow notes that public investments in America's mixed economy are largely bereft of public justification, except for the sake of promoting private enterprise (or national defense). But the *public* identity of investments in the civilian economy lacks a principled rationale:

> When government is asked to make these long-run social investments for capitalism, the requests are all ad hoc flying buttresses—essential to hold up the cathedral of capitalism but officially unrecognized. Being unrecognized they are not maintained and supported by capitalism. But when the public sector atrophies beyond some point, the flying buttresses fall, and the private cathedral falls with them.[20]

It is precisely this lack of a principled justification of the public sector's role in an inescapably mixed economy that focuses the ideological challenge at the end of this millennium. Capitalism by itself offers no such justification; indeed, capitalism is forever invoked to demean the public sector, even while capitalists seek to exploit public investments and preferments.

A free society undoubtedly needs *capitalists,* but a truly free society needs something grander and finer than *capitalism* for its identity and its public philosophy.

Nor does the pragmatic acknowledgment of a mixed economy do much for an ideological vision. Pragmatism and flexibility are certainly in order in maintaining the balance between public and private sectors, but the mere acceptance of the notion of a mixed economy does not by itself offer purposeful direction for government. There is no music or marching order in the idea of a mixed economy.

Francisco Weffort, a Brazilian political scientist at the University of São Paulo, candidly acknowledges the necessity of both strong central governments and vital markets—but with both subject to an even stronger civil society:

> Modern democratic society is not a society of the "minimal state," but on the contrary presupposes a strong state; at the same time, it also requires that civil society and democracy be strong enough to control the state. There is a permanent tension between the state and the market, but each needs the other. No modern democracy can either do without the market, as less thoughtful socialists claim, or get by with a "minimal state" of the sort that neoconservatives idealize.[21]

By what purposes and principles, then, will a necessarily strong state govern a modern society shaped by an inevitably mixed economy in which democratic politics and market economics remain in constant and confounding tension? That is a fundamental question of *political philosophy,* and not simply of economic theory—which is to say, it is a question of power and of justice more than it is a question of productivity or commerce.

The Obscurity of Power

A candid focus on the shapes of power and justice in American political economy can be obscured or avoided in a variety of ways.

One way is to presume that capitalist doctrine describes social reality, but it doesn't.

Another is to pretend that "democratic capitalism" is, or can be, a coherent social ethic—but it isn't, and it can't be.

A third way is to propose that the private, voluntary sector is capable of assuming the functions of the welfare state. In a tenth anniversary edition of their celebrated 1986 study, *Habits of the Heart,* sociologist Robert Bellah and his coauthors advance three compelling reasons why that is a fatuous proposal:

> The voluntary sector by no means has the resources to take up the slack, as churches and foundations have been pointing out repeatedly in recent years. The second reason is that our more affluent citizens may feel that they have fulfilled their obligation to society by giving time and money to "make a difference" through voluntary activity without considering that they have hardly made a dent in the real problems faced by most Americans. The third reason is that the voluntary sector is disproportionately run by our better off citizens, and a good many voluntary activities do more to protect the well-to-do than the needy.[22]

Communitarianism versus Individualism

Bellah and his colleagues continue to emphasize the potency and the antisocial consequences of "radical individualism" at the core of American ideology, so resurgent since 1980. The most serious consequence is a decline in the "social capital" generated by civic participation. Voluntary associations, labor unions, and political parties are all experiencing declining membership. Voter turnout has been trending downward for twenty years. Civil society is disintegrating.[23]

Among the prime challengers of radical individualism are communitarians of various persuasions—persons and groups promoting the normative principles of community and social responsibility. While communitarian ideas have a long history in religious and philosophical traditions, a new self-styled communitarian movement was launched in 1991 under the leadership of Amitai Etzioni, professor of social philosophy at George Washington University. Both *The Responsive Communitarian Platform: Rights and Responsibilities* (1991) and Etzioni's own book, *The Spirit of Community* (1993) emphasize the needs of children and families, the role of schools in moral education, the strengthening of neighborhood associations, civic responsibilities, and the reform of campaign finance—but mostly disavow endorsement of particular public policies.

In this contemporary form, the communitarian movement offers more a set of moral homilies than a political philosophy or ideological alternative. Etzioni's *Spirit of Community* is preoccupied with personal and family values and local institutions. Although advocating civic activism, Etzioni's view of government and politicians ("Washington is corrupt to the core") tends to reinforce the antigovernmental, antipolitical sentiments promoted by the Regressive Revolution. His attention to special interests is preoccupied with their financing of political action committees (PACs), to the neglect of their ideologies, think tanks, and propaganda. Perhaps in order to keep conservatives and liberals together, Etzioni avoids the basic issues of political economy altogether. Making common cause with conservative Harvard Law professor Mary Ann Glendon, author of *Rights Talk*, Etzioni implicitly disparages the effort to reconceive human rights as fundamental to political economy and social welfare. The "radical individualists" to whom he refers are not the aggressive Sunbelt entrepreneurs but the American Civil Liberties Union (ACLU) and other libertarians. And his own final appeal is individualistic and conversionist: "Change of heart is the most basic."[24]

This particular expression of communitarianism, in effect if not intention, has too much in common with the main themes of neoconservatism and voluntarism in obscuring or avoiding the shapes of power and justice in American political economy, and therefore contributes little to the imperatives of ideological renewal.

But communitarianism has long known other advocates and other viewpoints. My primary mentor in Christian social ethics, Walter Muelder of Boston University (now in his ninetieth year), is a lifelong communitarian. His 1972 response to writers of the Festschrift on his retirement was titled "Communitarian Christian Ethics." The communitarianism of Walter Muelder is wide and deep in its analytical and normative approaches to community in its most comprehensive senses: society as a whole, humankind as the ultimate unit of cooperation, realism about the ubiquity of government, sustained attention to the issues of power and justice in political economy.[25]

Some contemporary brands of communitarianism purport to offer radical alternatives to capitalism. Among democratic socialists, Michael Harrington and Gary Dorrien have proclaimed a pluralistic vision of socialism, with a nonstatist decentralization of authority (rather than national command economies), mixed forms of social ownership (featuring cooperative community-based enterprises and union sharing in corporate governing boards), and the dynamic role of the market (a system of "market socialism").[26]

While disavowing the socialist label, Gar Alperovitz of the National Center for Economic Alternatives similarly advocates a decentralized and pluralistic model of economic ownership and control. While he would support whatever legislative or regulatory reforms are politically doable at the national level, his basic strategy is local and long-range—to build up society "from below" by local community structures, neighborhood corporations, and worker-owned enterprises that nurture such fundamental values as democracy, liberty, and equality. Alperovitz is not disposed to spell out the political implications of such values for nationwide power structures.[27]

Appealing primarily to concerns for ecology and sustainability, process theologian John B. Cobb, Jr. has also joined the chorus of decentralizers, proposing a "community of communities" based on economically self-sufficient local and regional communities. Cobb dismisses capitalism for its "enormous disparities in wealth and power" and its ruthless commitment to impersonal market forces; he dismisses socialism for its preoccupation with "bureaucratic management." Both isms are faulted for their ecologically destructive commitments to "ideologies of growth" rather than sustainability.[28] Cobb offers a global vision of "earthism" that paradoxically invokes the traditional and localist Catholic principle of *subsidiarity:* higher levels should always defer first to lower levels. That is, political and economic decisions should be made at the smallest and most local levels possible. In Cobb's model, national and global authority would derive from cases only "when actions in one locale adversely affect others, or when what is needed requires a larger base to occur." Political authority should be transferred to larger "communities of communities" only insofar as "this is needed for the common good."[29] In effect, national governments and the United Nations are relegated to the status of institutions of last resort.

The Limits of Localism

Such bottom-up local-and-decentralized models of political economy, whether or not called "socialist," raise hard questions of political and social analysis, especially concerning the powers of national government. Since 1980, the Regressive Revolution has also been pushing decentralization—the devolution of the powers of government to state, local, and private responsibility. The great contradiction of the 1980s and 1990s is that, as the authority of the national government has been dismantled, deregulated, and decentralized, the powers of corporate business have been merged, conglomerated, pyramided, and multinationalized. In the process, many local communities have experienced a devastating loss of economic power to increasingly sovereign and remote corporate empires. So the question becomes: When are "radicals" (even socialists!) the unwitting accomplices of political regressives? How strong must the national state be to protect the possibilities of local autonomy? What ineluctable obligations belong to the national government to protect the basic human rights of citizens—even from the authority of state and local governments?

Even the most creative local economic initiatives and social projects are extremely vulnerable to national and international forces beyond their control. State and local tax bases are notoriously more regressive than national tax policies. Although mythology holds that state and local governments are "closer to the people," the reality is that those governments are more invisible than national government to most people and that voter turnout in state and local elections tends to be substantially lower. Most state legislatures are only part-time, with inadequate staff support.

In 1996 state governments were given the major responsibilities for welfare policy under the "welfare reform" (a deceitful misnomer!) enacted by the Republican Congress and signed by President Clinton. Abandoning a sixty-year national commitment to child welfare as a matter of children's rights, the legislation dismantled the federal safety net in favor of block grants to be administered by the states at their discretion. The folly and ultimately the cruelty of such block grant legislation were forecast in the findings of a recent study by the State Legislative Leaders Foundation. In most states,

> children's advocates are outgunned by richer and more powerful interests, whether homebuilders, truckers, nursing home operators, trial lawyers, veterans or the elderly. Children's advocates . . . have little or no access to the top legislative decision-makers. . . . Nobody who really knows the politics of most state capitols can seriously doubt what block grants would mean: a massive hemorrhage of protections and funds for children's and families' health care, child care, nutrition, income help and protective services.[30]

A further difficulty confronts the strategy of bottom-up political economy in local communities. The areas of greatest population growth are suburbs in metropolitan areas—municipalities in which community identity, participation, and political systems tend to be weak and to frustrate the creation of new community-based institutions. Moreover, the

residential patterns in metropolitan areas continue to reflect racial polarization. And it is suburbia that increasingly dominates most state legislatures.

None of this analysis is intended to discredit the creation and multi-
plication of local community-based and worker-owned enterprises
wherever feasible. Such ventures can do much to create normative
community itself, not least among diverse racial, cultural, and religious
groups.

The issue remains, however: What is the most promising and realistic
vision for the whole nation's political economy—and for the world political economy? And how will the national government define its responsibilities to both the public and private sectors, especially for the future of
today's children?

A Convivial Nation
in a Convivial World

The transformation of our ideological predicament of radical individualism, Business Mystique, capitalist triumphalism, and American exceptionalism clearly requires a set of communitarian principles of some
sort—but principles that comprehend the structures of power and justice
in national and international systems and therefore transcend local and
parochial notions of community.

In a 1968 address to the annual dinner of the Chicago Interseminary
Faculties Union (later published in *The Christian Century*), I began to
spell out such a set of communitarian perspectives for what I called a
"convivial theology"—an approach to world community as the context
for political imagination and the renewal of ideology.[31]

A convivial theology is much more than an appeal for festive feeling. It
calls for a new Christian humanism—an intellectual strategy, grounded
in Creation and Incarnation, for celebrating common humanity and the
universal work of Christ. The commitment to celebration is sacramental,
not self-indulgent—sacramental in reverence for our *convivium*, liter-
ally, "our living together."

In our *convivium*, all human beings are God's guests at the banquet of
life. And we are all created political animals—to share in the governance
of our common life-with-and-for-one-another. Politics is to be celebrated
as central to the plan and purposes of God's good creation. We share a
common citizenship in this *convivium* in which there is no *imperium*—
no political or economic or cultural or religious overlords. Our bodily life,
our material needs, our work, our production and distribution, our monetary and marketing relationships, within our society and among all

societies, are finally accountable to the common good, to principles of equity—and to the One who judges all people with equity.

Five years after my sketching this vision of a convivial theology, Ivan Illich enriched the vision in his book *Tools for Conviviality.*[32] For Illich, conviviality is an ethical concept for a truly civilized and humane common life not so driven by materialistic and industrial imperatives that persons are robbed of their autonomy and creativity. The authenticity of personal freedom is known only in conviviality—in the humanizing texture of interdependent communities and in harmony with the environment. Human life is redeemed by our liberation from the accumulation of material things and, most of all, by the nurture of our relationships.

Humanism:
Christian and Democratic

Conviviality in this at once sacramental and political sense helps to shape the ideological context of what I have called *democratic humanism.* What is offered here is certainly not a full-blown ideology. It is a provisional—always provisional—outline of the main themes that belong to a faithful ideology for American Christians.

The most basic warrant for democratic humanism is the defense of the good classical word *humanism* itself from its latest detractors, such as those self-proclaimed "evangelicals" who rail against "secular humanism." There is a highly proper theological sanction for humanism among Christians and Jews that insists that justice-as-lovingkindness is the highest obligation of religious faith. There is thus a theistic humanism, a godly humanism—and, for some, a Christian humanism embodied in the uncompromised humanity of the Incarnation of Jesus Christ.

The heritage of Christian humanism is not marginal to Christian history but central to it. Among Christian humanism's twentieth-century luminaries are Dietrich Bonhoeffer (who portrayed Jesus as "the man for others"); Jacques Maritain (author of *True Humanism,* described as "the humanism of the Incarnation"); the later Karl Barth (author of *The Humanity of God*); Paul Lehmann (whose theological ethics emphasized God's political action "to keep human life human"); Pope Paul VI (whose 1967 encyclical, *On the Development of Peoples,* celebrated a "transcendent humanism"); Harvey Cox (author of *The Secular City,* a manifesto of theological hope about the human future); and Gustavo Gutiérrez (whose *Theology of Liberation* viewed salvation as humanity's engagement "within an all-embracing salvific process" that "embraces the whole of man and all human history").

Democratic humanism obviously assumes democracy itself as the most humane form of politics, not simply on ideal principles but given both the ethical possibilities and the sinful proclivities of human nature. The dominant theological and philosophical voices in the shaping of U.S. constitutional government (notably James Madison) well understood these ambiguities of human nature as they bear on the exercise of political power—hence the hope for "a more perfect union," but a federal governmental system of separation of powers, checks and balances, respect for private property and commerce, and a Bill of Rights. A half century ago, Reinhold Niebuhr provided the succinct moral anthropology for democracy: "Man's capacity for justice makes democracy possible; but man's inclination to injustice makes democracy necessary."[33] Less often quoted but no less pertinent is Niebuhr's word that the "real point of contact between democracy and profound religion is in the spirit of humility which democracy requires and which must be one of the fruits of religion."[34] A more positive foundational principle common to both Christianity and democracy is the sacred dignity and equality of persons.

Such aphorisms of political theology, vital though they be, do not provoke much ideological controversy among Christians. It is when Christians proceed either to connect democratic politics with economic convictions, or even more to disconnect economics from democratic politics, that the real controversies erupt—and perhaps should erupt more often than they do!

A theologically grounded political ethic that is truly democratic will not subordinate that political term *democratic* to the status of a fig leaf for any economic ideology, whether capitalist or socialist or whatever. The basic texts and traditions of both capitalism and socialism—one individualistic, the other collectivist—tend to abstract from the wholeness of personhood-and-community, from the promise of conviviality. Both tend to put material things first. Humanism, rightly understood, at least means persons before things. It means community before property and profits. And it means politics before economics.

But democracy has more than a political definition. *The American Heritage Dictionary* helps us here by adding that democracy may mean "a social condition of equality and respect for the individual within the community"—a bit of conviviality right there in the dictionary! Because inequality is now being compounded in the American economy and society—and in much of the world's South and East—this wider vision of democracy sharply focuses the ideological challenge.

Democratic humanism ultimately requires *economic democracy,* without which political democracy is full of false promises. This means that equity in matters of power and participation is a fundamental, not a secondary, requirement of a humane economy.

It is strange indeed that the very idea of economic democracy should strike any of our contemporaries as a novel and perhaps dangerous idea.

However, it is an idea deeply rooted in American political and religious history. One of the earliest and most robust themes in American ideology was the egalitarian premise of Jeffersonian-Jacksonian principles of political economy, although its context was largely agrarian and preindustrial. Such egalitarianism did not reckon with the power structures of monopoly capitalism that developed after the Civil War.

Walter Rauschenbusch, premier theologian of the Social Gospel, offered a chapter simply titled "Economic Democracy" in his 1912 book, *Christianizing the Social Order,* in which he declared:

> Political democracy without economic democracy is an uncashed promissory note, a pot without the roast, a form without substance. . . . Economic democracy means more than the right of the organized workers to control their own industry. It means also the control of the people over their own livelihood. . . . Democracy means the absence of class rule; monopoly contains the essence of class rule.[35]

The rhetoric and much of the legislative substance of Franklin Roosevelt's New Deal appealed to economic democracy, even as they served to rescue capitalism from the threat of political extinction.

The term *economic democracy* returned once more to political discourse in the 1970s with the creation of a "Peoples' Bicentennial Commission" in 1976; Jeremy Rifkin's book *Own Your Own Job: Economic Democracy for Working Americans,* 1977; and Martin Carnoy and Derek Shearer's *Economic Democracy: The Challenge of the 1980s.* Common to these approaches are democratic participation in the workplace, employee ownership plans, and social control over capital investment.[36]

Democratic humanism emphasizes the foundational priority of human rights in all political and economic institutions. The great unfinished work of human rights in America is the naming and juridical articulation of economic and social rights, without which political rights may become forms without substance. The harsh reality for millions of Americans is that, while this nation has a human rights–based government, it does not yet have a human rights–based economy. "Democratic capitalism" is legitimated not by economic justice but only by political constitutions. Ethicist Beverly Harrison observes that basic economic functions such as "the production and distribution of food and housing or shelter, . . . health care delivery, education, and other essential goods and services are irrelevant to this discussion! . . . So long as the formal political rights . . . are present, . . . the economy is morally approved, whatever basic material conditions it sustains or effects."[37]

Since the 1930s, virtually every prominent advocate of economic democracy has proposed an economic bill of rights. President Franklin Roosevelt, in his January 11, 1944, State of the Union address, set forth "a second Bill of Rights under which a new basis of security and prosperity can be established for all." He included the right to a job; enough income for adequate food, clothing, and recreation; and

> The right of every family to a decent home;
>   The right to adequate medical care . . . ;
>   The right to adequate protection from the economic fears of old age,
>   sickness, accident, and unemployment;
>   The right to a good education.[38]

In 1983, three California scholar-activists authored a "new social contract" featuring a proposed ten-point "Economic Bill of Rights Resolution" for congressional action, endorsing the rights to the following:

1. a decent job for everyone willing to work

2. adequate health care

3. a good education

4. decent, affordable housing

5. old age protection through social security

6. nutritious food at a fair price

7. basic utilities (light, heat, telecommunications, transportation)

8. a clean, healthy environment

9. a secure and stable community

10. participation democratically in workplaces and government affairs.[39]

Similar proposals in the 1980s, provoked by escalating homelessness and federal retreat from social welfare and the cities, came from national church bodies. The National Conference of Catholic Bishops' 1986 pastoral letter, *Economic Justice for All,* affirmed "the rights to life, food, clothing, shelter, rest, medical care and basic education" as "indispensable to the protection of human dignity."[40] Referring to the constitutional heritage of civil and political rights, the bishops then declared: "We believe the time has come for a similar experiment in securing economic rights: the creation of an order that guarantees the minimum conditions of human dignity in the economic sphere for every person."[41] The next year, the United Church of Christ published a study document that, in explicitly espousing the concept of economic democracy, proposed an "Economic Bill of Rights" as an amendment to the U.S. Constitution, in the briefest possible wording: "The right of the people to access to employment, food, shelter, and health care should not be abridged."[42]

In an earlier chapter of this book, it was suggested that "any contemporary reconstruction of American ideology would do well to celebrate" the human rights tradition and its grounding in creation and covenant doctrines, and build upon it. One of the requisites of prophetic leadership in any nation is to lift up the most humane and liberating gifts of its heritage and reappropriate them for a vision of a better future. The idea of democracy's becoming, at last, economic democracy, and the appeal for an economic bill of rights do just that: they draw on what is most precious in the American heritage, and they offer this millennial generation's prophetic imperatives.

Reconstructing the Welfare State

Democratic humanism's imperatives of economic democracy, secured by juridical covenants to protect economic rights beyond property and commerce, ultimately must focus on *the reconstruction of the welfare state*. The very idea of the welfare state, especially for a nation whose Constitution's very first sentence promises to "promote the general welfare," needs to be redeemed from the pit of pejorative discourse. The shabbiness of much conservative and neoconservative rhetoric on welfare and the welfare state has relentlessly demeaned the victims of poverty and made humane public policy all but impossible. Such rhetoric has not only reduced "welfare" to a political cussword: it has virtually repudiated "entitlements" altogether. Such a repudiation risks the renunciation of all national standards and legal obligations—and ultimately economic rights—in the field of human welfare. But biblical scholar Walter Brueggemann reminds us that justice means we must "sort out what belongs to whom and return it to them. In this prophetic tradition, justice presumes social entitlements."[43]

A major part of this welfare default has to do with a minor part of what has constituted "welfare": Aid to Families with Dependent Children (AFDC). During the 1990s, AFDC funding averaged only 1 percent of the federal budget and only 3–4 percent of all U.S. social insurance costs. The median AFDC payment for a family of three was only about $4,400 a year in 1994, hardly a fortune.[44] But the bitter 1996 political battle over "welfare reform" was obsessed with this vital but minor fraction and ended with the abolition of AFDC, the federal guarantee of support for poor children. The public noise over AFDC drowned out concerns over federal largesse in what then-Secretary of Labor Robert Reich called "corporate welfare": subsidies and lax taxes dispensing tens of billions of dollars to businesses, even while federal tax, transportation, and housing policies have subsidized middle-class and suburban affluence. Welfare for corporations is promoted as investments in free enterprise and economic growth, whereas welfare for poor people is disparaged as "socialistic" and creating "dependency."

It is not the alleged excesses of the welfare state in behalf of the poor that is now the critical issue: It is the deficiencies of an incomplete welfare state that has yet to guarantee health insurance, employment security, and adequate support for schools, housing, transportation, and a clean environment in distressed urban and rural areas. In these late 1990s, the welfare state is not only incomplete and unreformed, but the "safety net" is being shredded by the harshness of simultaneous cutbacks in social programs by federal, state, and local governments. Millions of U.S. citizens are having to cope with cuts in welfare benefits, expiration of unemployment payments, reduced or unavailable rent subsidies, long waiting lists for public housing, shutdowns of health and community services, corporate termination of health insurance and pension plans. That this should be the case in the world's richest country is a national scandal shrieking for restitution.

Democratic humanism requires a welfare state strong enough to overcome the abuses and excessive self-aggrandizement of private principalities and powers that dehumanize the poor and obstruct the general welfare. It requires a natural, positive view of government as an order of God's good creation—a view that has not exactly been a vibrant article of faith for most American Christians since the early nineteenth century. However, there have been exceptional moments: in the Progressive and Social Gospel movements of the early twentieth century and in the brief spurts of social legislation in the mid-1930s and the mid-1960s.

James A. Nash has constructively (if brazenly) restated the case for "the goodness of government":

> Government is good! That is, civil government is not some "necessary evil" but rather an indispensable good. This is true not only of state and local governments but also of the federal government in the United States, and often especially the federal government. . . . The best government is not the one that governs least but the one that governs in proportionate response to public needs. Indeed, from some Christian and other religious perspectives, government is the blessing of God to meet these public needs.[45]

Strong government need not be inimical to human freedom and welfare; it is their prerequisite. Stephen L. Elkin, a University of Maryland political scientist writing in one of the constructive new journals of the 1990s titled *The Good Society,* declared that human liberty "is not a function of the absence of government or of a government small in scope, but the product of a well-designed government, one that prevents [special] interests with designs on the rights of the rest of the population from succeeding. The enemy of liberty is not government, but tyrannical and weak government."[46] Similarly, E. J. Dionne, Jr., has recently challenged the antigovernmental preachings of neoconservatives by his appeal for

> a fundamental philosophical defense of the promise of democratic government. . . . Politics and government cannot raise children, write love songs, create computer languages, invent the technology after the microchip or discover a cure for cancer. But politics and government do shape the conditions under which such acts of creativity are made easier or harder, more likely or less likely. Politics has everything to do with building a more just, more civil, more open society. Those who rallied to Progressivism, the cause of those who believe that democratic government has the capacity to improve society, always understood this. Their time has come again.[47]

That is a precious passage for democratic humanists.

For the years just ahead, a convivial agenda for reconstruction of the welfare state on the basis of democratic humanism might well include the following priorities:

1. guaranteed income (including pension security)
2. full employment (including work incentives)
3. basic education and job training
4. adequate child care for working parents
5. health insurance
6. tax reform (more progressive, fewer loopholes for the wealthy)

In the still larger meaning of the general welfare, major convivial priorities could include the following: substantial reductions in military spending, rehabilitation of urban infrastructures, upgrading railroads, strengthening preventive and rehabilitative policies in penal justice, a constitutional ban on capital punishment, political reforms in campaign finance and lobbying activities, and international trade practices that protect labor and environmental standards.

Democratic humanism will be pragmatic about the proportions of public-versus-private enterprise and control required to vindicate human rights and the common good. It will encourage every humane possibility of private initiative and enterprise. But it will not forever wait for profiteering ventures to do what, in fact, they will never do—that is, secure the most elemental standards of human living and the most redeeming gifts of civic culture for all the people.

The Challenge of Global Capitalism

Finally, democratic humanism is required by the increasing indivisibility of the whole human family, worldwide, in matters of economic and environmental welfare, as well as common security. Too much of the debate about economic policies continues to presuppose domesticated images of "the economy," while only adding on international issues as postscripts. If economic democracy is to be more than a domestic set of principles, the obligations of the world's richest and most powerful nations must be reformulated convivially. The efforts of a large majority of the world's governments in the 1970s to create a "New International Economic Order," under the auspices of the United Nations, were greeted mostly by scorn or neglect from the U.S. government. Those efforts, however, stemmed from the severe inequalities of power in the world economy in which the terms of trade, money, debt, investment, and technology transfer—particularly as they affect the poorer nations—had yet to become even topics of public debate in the United States. Nor had they become missional priorities for most of our churches. Nor have they yet.

The world economy today is largely shaped by the resurgent forces of laissez-faire Social Darwinism, most vividly embodied in the imperiously exploding power of transnational corporations beyond effective control by sovereign governments or intergovernmental institutions such as the United Nations. Global intergovernmental institutions are of two kinds: (1) those that reflect the overwhelming wealth and power of the major industrial nations of the North (such as the World Bank and the International Monetary Fund); and (2) those that are too weak to challenge or control the former (such as the United Nations Conference on Trade and Development [UNCTAD]).

An agenda for global economic democracy might well include the following:

1. Reversing the downward spiral of U.S. commitment to international development. The United States now ranks absolutely at the bottom—last among twenty-one aid providers in the percentage of its GDP devoted to foreign economic assistance, less than one-fifth of 1 percent (or 0.2 percent).

2. Solidifying the global revenue base for development, on the understanding that human rights require financial commitments beyond voluntarism and charity. A $50–$100 billion annual world development budget could be raised by a system of international taxation from sources proposed in United Nations discussion: (a) a global income tax, levied on

nations and progressively based on the per capita income of each country (with poorest nations exempt); (b) a global energy tax, such as $1 per barrel of oil; (c) a tax on the trade surpluses of surplus countries; (d) a tax on speculative international capital flows; and (e) a 10–20 percent allocation of the savings from a comprehensive program of reductions in military spending.

3. Restructuring the powers of international monetary institutions, especially the International Monetary Fund and the World Bank. For example, the voting strength of member nations ought to be based less on economic size and more on population.

4. Reshaping the relationships between aid providers and recipients so that they become genuine partnerships based on mutual planning rather than conditionalities imposed by providers.

5. Shifting the balance of economic assistance from loans to grants and debt forgiveness.

6. Shifting from the market fundamentalism of aid policies to a more pragmatic and flexible mix of public and private sector activity.

7. Promoting more equitable North-South trade through the World Trade Organization (WTO) and other bodies by establishing greater parity and stability of prices, ending price discrimination that imposes higher unit costs for products sold in the South, and curbing richer countries' subsidies for exports (especially agricultural exports) that tend to overwhelm competition from poor countries.

8. Developing more effective codes for the regulation of transnational corporations so that their investments do not promote tax evasion, substandard working conditions, and environmental devastation, or undermine the development planning of less-developed countries.

The overwhelming power of global capitalism at the end of this millennium presents perhaps the most serious of all ideological—and political and ethical—challenges to the American churches and to a convivial theology.

10

POLITICAL ECCLESIOLOGY: TOWARD A CONVIVIAL CHURCH

Christians have used beliefs about God and the world to undergird attitudes and actions with a highly problematic political import. First, Christians have deployed beliefs about God and the world to shore up the social and political status quo and thereby dampen any thought of the possibility or need for social or political change. . . . Second, Christians have used beliefs about God and the world to prevent the inequitable character of social and political relations from being seen as such. . . . Finally, Christians have employed beliefs about God and the world to hamper development of the attitudes necessary for outrage against injustice and sustained efforts to remedy it.

—Kathryn Tanner,
The Politics of God

The church is called to work for *shalom*—to be a laboratory of vital new community. . . . A crucial public role of North American churches is to think through and to embody a social vision for this time and place [and] to remove ideological blinders that, in overdeveloped Western societies, almost automatically subordinate social needs and ecosystems to the harsh requirements of market economic theory and practice.

—Dieter Hessel,
The Church's Public Role

So what is the church to do and to be about the challenges of ideology? For one thing, the renewal of ideology requires a transformation of American, especially Protestant, attitudes toward politics—and toward the mission of the church in the world of politics. If politics itself is excluded from the faith perspectives of Christians, they will hardly be persuaded that ideological reconstruction is an urgent religious task. Historically, Roman Catholics have been nurtured in a more humane and robust appreciation of the necessities of politics. And now many right-wing evangelicals have reversed their traditional aversion to mixing religion and politics and are doing the mixing with feverish intolerance—and in alliance with corporate chauvinists.

The theological grounding of politics in the purposes of God's good creation requires a new Christian vocabulary—a vocabulary that faithfully legitimizes, and faithfully chastens, the exercise of political power.

The renewal of ideology also requires a transformation of American, especially Protestant, attitudes toward intellect, which means overcoming at last the inane anti-intellectualism and downright mindlessness of so much of church life. Paul's powerful appeal for a new life in Christ, addressed originally to "all God's beloved in Rome," includes this directive no less appropriate to all God's beloved in America: "Do not be conformed to this world, but be transformed by the renewing of your minds, so that you may discern what is the will of God" (Rom 12:2).

The discernment of what is ethical in the complex social and technical realities of national and international life indeed requires an unabashed and robust intellectuality, albeit an intellectuality steeped in prayer and compassion.

These twin defaults, antipolitics and anti-intellectualism—so vitiating of the moral and spiritual life of Christians and their churches—must be confessed and directly confronted in any convivial strategy for the renewing of our minds ideologically.

Since the 1960s, there has been some circulation of the term *political theology;* a term associated with the German Catholic theologian J. B. Metz and with various liberation theologians. But it is a term still new and strange (if not indecent!) to too many American Protestant ears and eyes. Political theology rightly refers to the attributes of power, action, justice, and peace in the most basic Christian beliefs—beliefs about God and Christ and Spirit and church. Political theology is foundational for ideology but not identical with it. Political theology's claims about divinity cannot be exclusively claimed for any particular political or economic philosophy.

The new vocabulary of political theology must be enriched by such terms as *political hermeneutics, political ecclesiology, political ministry*, and *political ideology.*

We surely need a *political hermeneutic* if we are to claim biblical foundations for political theology. That is, we need an orientation to scripture that interprets political life faithfully and credibly in biblical categories—not to say we may proof-text our own partisan opinions and policies. This is to recognize that politics was not an unfamiliar subject to biblical writers. More than seventy years ago, Clarence True Wilson wrote:

> The Old Testament from Pentateuch to the Prophets was a book of politics.
> The books of Moses were law books; Genesis was the history leading up to
> the founding of a nation; Leviticus was a law book both for the nation and
> the Church; Numbers is a story of a national census and a division of the
> tribes; Deuteronomy was a revision and codification of the national law. . . .
> The Prophets were reformers, preachers of civic righteousness who mixed
> into everything, rebuked kings, reformed abuses, regimented society,
> preached civic virtue.[1]

While some Christians have attempted to de-politicize the New Testament, the gospel Jesus preached called for national transformation, not just individual conversion. That gospel led Jesus to confront public issues at the power center of his nation, as well as Roman imperialism—and that gospel cost him his life. The Crucifixion was a political event before it became the transcendent symbol of Christian faith. And the Resurrection proved that such faith could convert governments and outlast empires.

If we presume that the church has a mission of any kind at all in public affairs, we need a well-wrought body of doctrine that both impels and tempers that mission—a *political ecclesiology* that defines the church's public ministry. The core of such doctrine is suggested by Joseph Allen's "covenantal model" of Christian ethics. The church, according to Allen, is the special covenant that witnesses to God's inclusive covenant of love and justice. The inclusive covenant is "the whole body of God's children, all of whom God loves. . . . All matter alike in God's sight, not only those who confess faith through Jesus Christ. . . . All people are members [with] responsibilities to and for one another, and corresponding needs and human rights."[2] Such a political ecclesiology proclaims a church that is convivial within its own fellowship even as it serves the God-given conviviality of the whole human family.

If we believe that both clergy and laity have appropriate political roles to play, we must exalt politics as a Christian vocation and conceive its responsibilities as a *political ministry*. That term, political ministry, has been most fruitfully developed and interpreted by the Catholic sisterhoods sharing in Network, a justice and peace lobby based in Washington.

If we recognize that there is no escape from basic beliefs in the public struggles over political economy—the connections between public and private power structures—and the relationships of nations and races, we must articulate a *political ideology*, remembering, of course, that Christian faith cannot be absolutely identified with any particular ideology, but that "wrestling with principalities and powers" means the power to challenge unjust ideas with clearly expressed beliefs of our own.

A church with a convivial theology will possess a political ecclesiology that concretely defines specific contributions of the church to political life. This book concludes with a ten-point outline of such contributions.

1. *The convivial church will engage its members in styles of action and reflection most conducive to the formation of political beliefs that are well-grounded in their Christian faith.*

Ideological formation and commitment are most fruitfully nurtured in the arenas of political action—provided time and opportunity are created for analysis and reflection. Such a priority on the tutelage of action is contrary to most prevailing models of Christian education and formation—models that assume that Christian nurture must precede social involvement, or even that such nurture can proceed without requiring any social involvement. It is a special contribution of liberation theology to expose such models as based on bad psychology and, even more, bad theology. Gustavo Gutiérrez defined theology as "critical reflection on Christian praxis"; the "presence and action of the Christian in the world." *Praxis* includes the practical life and experience of the church itself but especially means going "beyond the visible boundaries" of the church into the secular arena.[3] If theology itself requires engagement in political action, surely ideological formation requires it.

The churches are full of people who are forever getting nurtured while forever postponing their involvement or avoiding involvement altogether. Christian preaching and teaching which presuppose that church folk can learn much about the meaning of discipleship without struggling with principalities and powers in the world are shallow indeed; they are infected with what Dietrich Bonhoeffer called "cheap grace." The most genuinely spiritual congregations I know are those whose members bring to their worship the burdens of their witness in the world, their costly discipleship.

2. *The convivial church will provide an open forum for discussion of the most controversial issues that affect the well-being of the people in the community, the nation, and the world.*

Some misguided Christians insist that the church is the last place such controversies should be allowed expression. The convivial church will insist on precisely the opposite—that (at least for Christians), the church should be the first place where the people's well-being is discussed, even and especially if controversy is involved. In too many congregations and other Christian gatherings, many persons do not feel free to express their honest convictions for fear of inviting spiritual repression, moral indignation, or social isolation. Too many Christians actually engaged in social action through nonchurch organizations testify that it is more difficult to be honest in church than in those other organizations. The convivial church will learn to welcome and even celebrate controversy over significant issues, even in the sanctuary as an act of worship. A convivial political ecclesiology will constantly invite and welcome dissent and diversity in the intramural political life of church institutions at all levels.

3. *The convivial church will help shape public policy debate on the crucial issues of justice and peace.*

It will do so through the testimony of individual members, but also through the corporate witness of official church bodies (congregational, denominational, ecumenical) and of various parachurch groups and coalitions. In fact, the most significant consequence of corporate witness typically is not the direct impact of a church pronouncement or study document on public policy but the process of formulation that engages hosts of individual members. The two pastoral letters of the U.S. Catholic bishops in the 1980s (*The Challenge of Peace* and *Economic Justice for All*) and the 1986 pastoral letter of the United Methodist bishops (*In Defense of Creation*) were especially notable for engaging many thousands of church members in two-year preparatory processes.

Helping to shape the policy debate may mean advocacy of a particular law or treaty, or proposing a new, alternative policy, or criticizing the moral arguments or assumptions of policy options. The church as such can seldom claim the greatest technical expertise, but its testimony is made credible to the extent the church makes use of its members with vocational competence. And the convivial church will always insist that no area of policy is purely technical; all policies are shot through with ethical dimensions.

Christians engaged in public discourse must be able to speak three languages: (1) the language of Christian faith when their confessional beliefs are clearly at stake and can be expressed without intolerance for other confessions; (2) the language of common faith with non-Christian religious groups; and (3) a common civic language expressing humane concerns without theological invocations. Knowing which language to speak at a particular moment is a matter of interfaith and civic sensitivity, but also of appropriate modesty and respect for opposing views.

4. *The convivial church will expose the ideological assumptions underlying public policy.*

For the United States at the end of this millennium, the endurance of antigovernment capitalist dogma across most of the policy agenda, both domestic and foreign, is a reality that must be named by the church. The following examples document that reality:

> To the political and professional groups dominating health policy, health care remains a profitable commodity in a private enterprise economy rather than a matter of human right and the general welfare.
>
> Notwithstanding a principled U.S. commitment to full employment dating back to 1946, public sector jobs are often politically scorned as "make-work" and demeaning, even in the face of rapidly disintegrating urban infrastructures, decaying bridges, deteriorating public schools, and a severe shortage of decent low-income housing, all of which clamor for public investment and the employment of many jobless persons.
>
> Some of the "structural adjustment programs" of the International Monetary Fund, designed to cope with the debt crises of less-developed countries (but unhappily acronymed

"SAPS"), have typically forced African countries to devalue their currency, sacrifice subsistence crops for export earnings, curb workers' wages and subsidies while prices are rising, curtail public investment in health and infrastructure, facilitate investment and economic control by foreign corporations, and thereby serve as scourges by the global capitalist market, even as they compound the poverty and political oppression of the countries they purport to help.

5. *The convivial church will provide alternative intelligence systems for both domestic and foreign policy.*

The church's congregational and pastoral life affords unique vantage points for understanding and interpreting the impact of public policies on individuals, families, and communities—and their physical and mental health, moral standards, social attitudes, and sentiments toward government. In this engagement with the lives and livelihoods of its members and neighbors, the church discovers that there is no great gulf between its pastoral and prophetic ministries. There is no "zero-sum game" between the two, as if being more pastoral could possibly mean being less prophetic. No, to be truly pastoral is to be immersed in the social contexts in which personal and family lives are cast, and then to interpret these contexts to those with the power to transform them.

The church's missionary, transnational life affords an intimate engagement in the communities, cultures, and economies of other nations that often far exceeds the outreach of U.S. government personnel, especially in the poorest of countries. That engagement makes possible public testimony that supplements, corrects, or challenges official foreign policies too often tied to the viewpoints of economic and military elites. At times, it requires a willingness to name the untruths in official rhetoric and reports. In recent years, the church's intelligence on Central American and Southern Africa has effectively challenged and helped to reorient U.S. policies. Such intelligence can be much more than an alternative data-base; it can develop into an alternative understanding of political and economic systems, a framework for ideological reconstruction.

6. *The convivial church will serve as an advocate for people who are unrepresented or underrepresented in the political system.*

Given the political power and ideological sway of Big Money, America's poorest people in both inner cities and rural areas are the regular losers in the nation's public policies, and women and children are disproportionately the losers among the poor. Racial and ethnic minorities' long, bitter, unfinished struggles for equality have lately been freshly obstructed by anti–civil rights, economic, and welfare policies of the Regressive Revolution. The church must know all it can know about the sufferings and oppressions of marginalized persons and groups—and about the systemic causes of their distress—and speak truth to the powers that can help redeem their predicament.

Every one of the world's nations is a de facto constituency for the United States, given the pervasiveness and intrusiveness of American power—political, military, economic, cultural—on every continent. Decisions made or neglected in Washington, D.C., concerning interest rates, immigration, agriculture, environment, energy, nuclear weapons, land mines, covert intelligence operations, drug control, seabed mining, world trade, the World Bank, United Nations peacekeeping all have decisive impact on the life and death realities of other countries. The diplomatic representatives of the world's poorest countries typically have little influence on such decisions. The needs and hurts of their peoples tend to be invisible to the American public. They seldom surface as priority issues in election campaigns or congressional debates.

The convivial church will speak for the well-being of the whole human family, especially for those peoples effectively disfranchised by imperious patterns of political and economic power. Such a church will understand and interpret the dogmas of economic and military policy that tend to dehumanize millions of citizens the world over. And such a church will be the advocate for those new institutions of global governance essential to physical well-being, common security, and ecological sustainability.

7. *The convivial church will provide a sanctuary for the victims and targets of political oppression.*

One of the imperative functions of the church in and for the world is to offer a shelter from the conflicts and injustices of the world.

> The *koinonia,* the loving community, lifts itself above all hostilities to minister to both the participants in and the victims of violence. The community of faith is a fellowship of peril and hope which always, as John Bennett puts it, affords its members "a home, where in perplexity or under pressure from hostile forces they may find both light and healing." Faithful Christianity must always transcend political struggles even while identifying deeply and relevantly with them.[4]

The function of sanctuary, however, is not limited to church members. It has embraced slaves, Jews, conscientious objectors, exiles from Southeast Asia, refugees from Central America, West Africa, and many other places.

In the process of providing sanctuary, the church renews its loyalty to a Sovereign above all national claims to sovereignty and reaffirms its radical commitment to human freedom as God's greatest gift. Paul wrote to the Galatians: "For freedom Christ has set us free" (Gal. 5:1). Such freedom is essential to our very humanity, but such freedom is to be shared with others in the love and peace of Christ. It is a convivial gift. To provide a sanctuary is to keep alive the very possibility of freedom for those who might otherwise lose it, if not their very lives.

8. *The convivial church will work to strengthen the moral resources of parallel institutions that also shape public values.*

The church has no monopoly on the formation of beliefs and values that constitute ideologies. Education at all levels, as previously noted, has become a prime ideological battleground for the Regressive Revolution. How the public schools, colleges, and universities teach the knowledge and issues of history, culture, race, and gender; orient their students to the nature and workings of government and politics; cope with the Business Mystique and pressures toward competitiveness, militarism, and privatization; permit or manipulate religious topics: these are matters crying for Christian engagement if ideological reconstruction is to have a chance. At the local community level, convivial Christians must be well-organized to contend with the Christian Coalition and other regressive groups seeking to dominate school and library boards and to control curricula.

Similarly, prospects for the nurture of convivial convictions are profoundly affected by the print and broadcast media, their news coverage, political messages, entertainment, treatment of religion, and, not least, advertising. Private corporate ownership of most of the media makes them heavily profit-oriented and therefore powerful adjuncts to capitalist ideology. The fusion of well-funded right-wing religion with right-wing politics in both television and radio provides a particularly formidable challenge to more progressive voices. The media are the principal purveyors of the grossest consumptionist values and the public's obsessions with violence and raw sexuality, both in news coverage and entertainment. Those same obsessions continue to corrupt the movie industry. Here it must be acknowledged that right-wing groups have been more vocal than others in condemning the most sordid entertainment. Altogether, the mainline churches have yet to contrive a powerful media strategy for the formation of a more convivial society.

A basic question of political ecclesiology is at stake in the church's struggle with these parallel value-shaping institutions: Will the church pretend to a sectarian monopoly of redeeming values and thereby stand aside from the struggle for power over the shaping of culture? Or will the church act on the understanding that God is indeed at work outside the church as well as within, and that every cultural institution has become an arena of conflict between convivial and regressive forces? The latter have ostentatiously and often viciously declared their culture wars and appear to be winning on many fronts.

9. *The convivial church will celebrate politics and government service as Christian vocations second to none in their sacred significance.*

The antipolitical animus of what H. Mark Roelofs calls "the

Protestant/Bourgeois Complex" falls with particular contempt on those who have chosen public service as a career, most especially legislators, party leaders, and civil servants.[5] "Politician" and "bureaucrat" are more commonly terms of opprobrium than of honor. All too often, it is the rhetoric of self-righteous Christians (even of Christian politicians pretending to be nonpolitical) that leads the chorus of disdain for politicians and government employees.

In a lifetime of ministry constantly implicated in relationships with practitioners and scholars of politics, I must testify that my pantheon of Christian saints is filled by at least as many politicians as preachers—men and women graced by consecrated vocations for justice and peace, by audacity in the face of fierce opposition, and by faithfulness in the wake of recurring defeats. Public service is one of the most exposed vocations in our society—and rightly so in a democratic society—which means its sins are more visible than those of other professions, including business, medicine, and the clergy (although exposure of clergy sins seems to be catching up a bit). A recent letter from a lifelong politician and government executive referred to my oft-repeated word that "politics is holy ground" and then testified that it "has been an inspiration and guiding light" to him since he first heard it, adding that he often quotes it "to those who are inclined to ignore, scoff at, or revile politics."

The title of a wonderful, well-humored memoir, *Politics Is My Parish,* highlights the extraordinary, saintly public service of Brooks Hays, the Arkansas congressman, United Nations delegate, and president of the Southern Baptist Convention whose courage on civil rights cost him his congressional seat in a 1958 election at the height of the Little Rock desegregation controversy. Hays, who died in 1981, followed his electoral defeat with appointments as assistant secretary of state and adviser to two presidents, but also election as a vice-president of the National Council of Churches and selection as director of the Ecumenical Institute at Wake Forest University. Hays's memoir contains a chapter on "Quest for a Vocation" that recounts his student struggle to decide between ordained ministry and a profession in law and politics. A long conversation with a Lutheran pastor helped to exalt the option for politics:

> We spent an evening together and he did help me. Not by reaching any categorical judgment about what I ought to do with my life, but by interpreting the spiritual and moral aspects of a political course, if I should finally be drawn in that direction. As a professional churchman, he convinced me that there are many parishes for one who wants to utilize his talents in useful and gratifying ways, and that politics may be on a par with the Christian ministry, depending, of course, on how it is pursued. He was quite sure that if I chose a political career I could view it as a parish. . . . I am heavily in his debt for counsel and encouragement in a difficult and crucial stage of life.[6]

We will never know what Brooks Hays might have accomplished as a clergyman, but we can praise God for all that he accomplished as a politician and Christian layman.

The work of ideological reconstruction should not be monopolized by philosophers, theologians, social scientists, and other academies; it must include persons whose vocations disclose both the possibilities and limitations of government.

10. *The convivial church will challenge all its members to confess, reconstruct, and continually renew their own ideologies in the light of Christian faith.*

That challenge means looking at *the world that is* with fresh eyes and then visioning *the world that might be* with the faithful eyes of hope and love.

One of the direst institutional weaknesses in American churches is the languid ministry of adult education and its implications for the ministry of the laity in the world outside the church. More and more laity have attained levels of education and professional sophistication that position them for significant Christian leadership in society. Too much of the church's adult education—even where it exists at all—fails to rise to that level of lay intelligence and experience, let alone stretch lay minds beyond it. At the same time, laity have become increasingly oriented to the politics of work—or, more familiarly, "special interests." The politics of work in America is much too captivated by the self-aggrandizing dogmas of individualism and the Business Mystique.

Adult education in the church requires a new vocational strategy that focuses on the public responsibilities of every profession and equips the laity to think and rethink their vision of the good society. Such a strategy would reverse the habitual domestication of the laity that results from preoccupation with the church's intramural maintenance and private pieties—a domestication that fails to confront the systemic and ideological barriers to justice and peace.

In a 1966 classic provocatively titled *The Church Inside Out*, Johannes Hoekendijk lamented the chronic tendency of American churches to create "church-domesticated laity, tamed and caged by the church" instead of being empowered for their apostolate of work and citizenship in the world.[7] A World Council of Churches report on the same theme, *The Church for Others*, declared:

> The Church lives in order that the world may know its true being. It is *pars pro toto;* it is the first fruits of the new creation. But its centre lies outside itself; it must live "ex-centredly." It has to seek out those situations in the world that call for loving responsibility and there it must announce and

point to *shalom*. This ex-centric position of the Church implies that we must stop thinking from the inside towards the outside.[8]

Political ecclesiology means turning the church inside out.

A new vocational strategy of adult education ought not assume that every congregation should work at the renewal of ideology entirely by itself, especially in view of the demographic limits of most congregations. Several churches together, or a presbytery or diocese or district, or a council of churches might provide the most auspicious structure, in partnership with wider ecumenical and denominational organizations, colleges, and seminaries.

In this richest country in the world, shamed as it is by the extent of poverty within its borders as well as the poverty that it compounds on other continents, there is yet another scandalous form of poverty—*the poverty of political imagination.* The most common themes of public discourse seldom really touch "the better angels of our nature" (to quote Lincoln), spiritually or ethically. They are severely lacking in the deepest communitarian values. They fail to offer well-wrought visions of the convivial world promised by the prophets.

Here and there, the convivial church will create *academies of political imagination*—places devoted to expectations of a world made new. The participants in such academies, whether real live politicians or other laity-or-clergy-in-process-of-formation-as-politicians, must be willing to invest themselves in a uniquely personal process of creativity in which they work out their own political salvation, even while engaging each other in the friction that fires up new ideas, and even while involving themselves directly in political struggle. Such academies must invite persons of the most diverse political, vocational, racial, ethnic, national, and faith identities so that Christian imagination may be enriched and tempered by experiencing the other sides of many forms of dialogue.

The agenda for such dialogues will not be trivial. It will lift up the kinds of topics suggested in chapter 8: God's action in history, moral anthropology, basic social institutions, the world of nations, the moral burdens of history, violence and nonviolence, a vision of the future, and political ecclesiology itself.

Who knows? Out of such dialogues in many places, in this and other nations, a new movement and a new widely shared vision—a profoundly humanistic, spirit-filled vision—might emerge. And if it should emerge and catch the imagination and then the commitment of a sufficient number of persons empowered by the vision—

> Then shall all shackles fall; the stormy clangor
> Of wild war-music o'er the earth shall cease;
> Love shall tread out the baleful fire of anger,
> And in its ashes plant the tree of peace.[9]

NOTES

Chapter 1:
The Inevitability of Ideology

1. George F. Will, "An Eisenhower Fantasy," *The Washington Post,* April 16, 1995, C7.
2. James Davison Hunter, *Culture Wars: The Struggle to Define America* (New York: Basic Books, 1991).
3. Robert Kuttner, "Divided, We Stand a Chance," *The Washington Post,* July 23, 1995, C9.
4. Jessica Mathews, "The U.N.'s Next 50 Years," *The Washington Post,* January 17, 1995, A19.

Chapter 2:
The Idea of Ideology

1. Robert Haber, "The End of Ideology as Ideology," in *The End of Ideology Debate,* ed. Chaim I. Waxman (New York: Simon & Schuster, 1968), 187.
2. José Míguez Bonino, *Toward a Christian Political Ethics* (Philadelphia: Fortress Press, 1983), 82–83.
3. David McLellan, *Ideology* (Minneapolis: University of Minnesota Press, 1986), 5–6.
4. Vladimir Lenin, *What Is to Be Done?,* quoted in McLellan, *Ideology,* 25.
5. Antonio Gramsci, *Prison Notebooks,* quoted in McLellan, *Ideology,* 29.
6. Karl Mannheim, *Ideology and Utopia* (New York: Harcourt, Brace & Co., 1936), 77.
7. Ibid.
8. Ibid., 192.
9. Ibid., 194.
10. Ibid., 212.
11. Ibid., 229.
12. Ibid., 231–32.
13. Ibid., 240.
14. Ibid., 250.
15. Ibid., 262–63.

16. Rubem Alves, quoted in editorial,"The Resurrection of Utopia," *The Christian Century,* March 25, 1970, 347.
17. Gustavo Gutiérrez, *A Theology of Liberation: History, Politics and Salvation,* trans. and ed. Caridad Inda and John Eagleson (Maryknoll, N.Y.: Orbis Books, 1973), 232–39.

Chapter 3:
The Denial of Ideology in America

1. Harold Lasswell, *Politics: Who Gets What, When, and How* (New York: McGraw-Hill, 1936).
2. Michael Harrington, *Toward a Democratic Left* (Baltimore: Penguin Books, 1969), 4–5.
3. Ibid., 246.
4. John F. Kennedy, quoted in Peter Steinfels, *The Neoconservatives: The Men Who Are Changing America's Politics* (New York: Simon & Schuster, 1979), 42.
5. Thomas W. Braden, "I'm Glad the CIA Is 'Immoral,' " *The Saturday Evening Post,* May 20, 1967, 10. Quoted in Steinfels, *The Neoconservatives,* 84.
6. Edward Shils, "The End of Ideology?" in *The End of Ideology Debate,* ed. Chaim I. Waxman (New York: Simon & Schuster, 1968), 60.
7. Ibid., 61.
8. Seymour Martin Lipset, *Political Man: The Social Bases of Politics* (Garden City, N.Y.: Doubleday & Co., 1960), 406.
9. Daniel Bell, "The End of Ideology in the West," in *The End of Ideology Debate,* ed. Chaim I. Waxman (New York: Simon & Schuster, 1968), 88.
10. Ibid., 99.
11. Ibid., 88.
12. Hannah Arendt, *The Origins of Totalitarianism* (New York: Harcourt, Brace, Jovanovich, 1973), 469–71.
13. David Walsh, *After Ideology: Recovering the Spiritual Foundations of Freedom* (Washington, D.C.: Catholic University Press, 1995), 248.
14. Ibid., 273.
15. Nicholas Lossky et al., eds., *Dictionary of the Ecumenical Movement* (Geneva: World Council of Churches Publications, 1991), 500.
16. Ibid.
17. Reinhold Niebuhr, *Christian Realism and Political Problems* (New York: Charles Scribner's Sons, 1953), 14.
18. Reinhold Niebuhr, *An Interpretation of Christian Ethics* (New York: Meridian Books, 1956), 26. Originally published by Harper & Brothers, 1935.
19. Jim Wallis, *The Soul of Politics* (Maryknoll, N.Y.: Orbis Books, 1994), 22.
20. Ibid., xviii.
21. Ibid., 22–23.
22. Ibid., xxii.
23. Ibid., 44.
24. Ibid., xxiv.

Chapter 4:
The Reality of Ideology in America

1. Ernest Lee Tuveson, *Redeemer Nation: The Idea of America's Millennial Role* (Chicago: University of Chicago Press, 1968).
2. Robert N. Bellah, "Civil Religion in America," *Daedalus* (Winter 1967): 8, 18, 19.
3. Martin E. Marty, *The Public Church: Mainline-Evangelical-Catholic* (New York: Crossroad, 1981), 16–17.
4. H. Mark Roelofs, *The Poverty of American Politics* (Philadelphia: Temple University Press, 1992), 1–2.
5. Ibid., 24.
6. Alexis de Tocqueville, *Democracy in America,* 2 vols. (New York: Vintage Books, 1956), 1:325.
7. Reinhold Niebuhr, *Pious and Secular America* (New York: Charles Scribner's Sons, 1958), 1–2.
8. James K. Polk, "Inaugural Address, March 4, 1845," in *Messages and Papers of the Presidents,* ed. James D. Richardson (Washington, D.C., 1897), 4:381.
9. Samuel Huntington, *American Politics: The Promise of Disharmony* (Cambridge: Harvard University Press, 1981), 33.
10. Perry Miller, *The New England Mind: The Seventeenth Century* (New York: Macmillan Co., 1939), 418–19.
11. Warren R. Copeland, *And the Poor Get Welfare: The Ethics of Poverty in the United States* (Nashville: Abingdon Press, 1994), 122.
12. Richard Hofstadter, *The Age of Reform* (New York: Vintage Books, 1955), 45–46.
13. James Madison, *The Federalist Papers,* no. 51 (New York: The New American Library, 1961), 322.
14. Richard Hofstadter, *Anti-Intellectualism in American Life* (New York: Vintage Books, 1966), 237.
15. Hofstadter, *The Age of Reform,* 39–40.
16. Roelofs, *The Poverty of American Politics,* 217.
17. Ibid., 218.

Chapter 5:
The Regressive Revolution I: Antistatism

1. Peter Steinfels, *The Neoconservatives: The Men Who Are Changing America's Politics* (New York: Simon & Schuster, 1979); Sidney Blumenthal, *The Rise of the Counter-Establishment: From Conservative Ideology to Political Power* (New York: Times Books, 1986); Gary Dorrien, *The Neoconservative Mind* (Philadelphia: Temple University Press, 1993).
2. Steinfels, *The Neoconservatives,* 1.
3. Ibid., 294.
4. Leon Howell, "Funding the War of Ideas," *The Christian Century,* July 19–26, 1995, 701.

5. James Davison Hunter, *Culture Wars: The Struggle to Define America* (New York: Basic Books, 1991), 111.

6. Richard Weaver, *Ideas Have Consequences* (Chicago: University of Chicago Press, 1948).

7. Robert Paul Wolff, *"1984" Revisited* (New York: Alfred A. Knopf, 1973), 9.

8. Blumenthal, *The Rise of Counter-Establishment,* 75.

9. Jude Wanniski, quoted in Blumenthal, *The Rise of the Counter-Establishment,* 171.

10. Leslie Lenkowsky, quoted in Blumenthal, *The Rise of the Counter-Establishment,* 194–95.

11. George Gilder, quoted in Blumenthal, *The Rise of the Counter Establishment,* 205.

12. George Gilder, *Wealth and Poverty* (New York: Bantam Books, 1982), 7, 82.

13. Ibid., 315.

14. John Schwarz, *America's Hidden Success: A Reassessment of Twenty Years of Public Policy* (New York: W. W. Norton, 1983), 76–77. The contrast between alternative readings of the history of public policy was a main theme in my 1985 presidential address for the Society of Christian Ethics, "Politics and the Ethics of History," published in *The Annual: The Society of Christian Ethics 1985* (Washington, D.C.: Georgetown University Press, 1986), 3–17. See also Charles Murray, *Losing Ground: American Social Policy, 1950–1980* (New York: Basic Books, 1984).

15. Allen Hunter, quoted in Michael W. Apple, "Ideology, Equality, and the New Right," in *The Challenge of Pluralism,* ed. F. Clark Power and Daniel K. Lapsley (Notre Dame: University of Notre Dame Press, 1992), 55.

16. Sheldon Wolin, "The New Conservatives," *New York Review of Books,* February 5, 1976, 8. Quoted in Steinfels, *The Neoconservatives,* 17.

17. Dorrien, *The Neoconservative Mind,* 384.

18. Lester Thurow, *The Future of Capitalism* (New York: William Morrow, 1996), 33.

19. Norman Podhoretz, "The Disaster of Women's Lib," *New York Post,* August 18, 1987. Quoted in Dorrien, *The Neoconservative Mind,* 352, 355.

20. *The Common Good: Social Welfare and the American Future* (New York: Ford Foundation, 1989).

21. E. J. Dionne, Jr., "The Liberal Revival," *The Washington Post,* February 4, 1996, C1, C4.

22. Ralph Reed, *Policy Review,* Summer 1993. Quoted in Dan Balz and Ronald Brownstein, "God's Fixer," *The Washington Post Magazine,* January 28, 1996, 25–28.

Chapter 6:
The Regressive Revolution II: Anticommunism and After

1. Gary Dorrien, *The Neoconservative Mind* (Philadelphia: Temple University Press, 1993), ix.

2. Irving Kristol, quoted in Sidney Blumenthal, *The Rise of the Counter-Estab-*

lishment: From Conservative Ideology to Political Power (New York: Times Books, 1986), 148.

3. Dorrien, *The Neoconservative Mind,* 182.
4. John Silber, *Straight Shooting* (New York: Harper & Row, 1989), 296, 303.
5. Norman Podhoretz, quoted in Blumenthal, *The Rise of the Counter-Establishment,* 308.
6. George F. Kennan, *At a Century's Ending: Reflections 1982–1995* (New York: W. W. Norton, 1996), 186–87.
7. *The Common Good: Social Welfare and the American Future* (New York: Ford Foundation, 1989).
8. Dorrien, *The Neoconservative Mind,* 323.
9. E. J. Dionne, Jr., "Back to the Future," *The Washington Post Magazine,* January 28, 1996, 28.
10. Ibid., 30.
11. Charles Krauthammer, quoted in Dorrien, *The Neoconservative Mind,* 331.
12. Joshua Muravchik, "Affording Foreign Policy," *Foreign Affairs,* March/April 1996, 13.
13. Michael Novak, quoted in Dorrien, *The Neoconservative Mind,* 339.
14. Ben Wattenberg, quoted in Dorrien, *The Neoconservative Mind,* 327.
15. Patrick Buchanan, "American First—And Second, And Third," *The National Interest,* Spring 1990, 81. Quoted in Dorrien, *The Neoconservative Mind,* 342–43.

Chapter 7:
Churches in the Ideological Struggle

1. Michael Novak, quoted in Leon Howell, *Funding the War of Ideas* (Cleveland: United Church Board for Homeland Ministries, 1995), 50.
2. Michael Novak, *The Spirit of Democratic Capitalism* (New York: Simon & Schuster, 1982) and *The Catholic Ethic and the Spirit of Capitalism* (New York: Free Press, 1993); George Weigel, "American Catholicism and the Capitalist Ethic," in *The Capitalist Spirit: Toward a Religious Ethic of Wealth Creation,* ed. Peter Berger (San Francisco: ICS Press, 1990); Richard John Neuhaus, *Doing Well and Doing Good: The Challenge to the Christian Capitalist* (New York: Doubleday & Co., 1992).
3. Michael Novak, *Toward a Theology of the Corporation* (Washington, D.C.: American Enterprise Institute, 1981), 9.
4. Ibid., 33.
5. Ibid., 37–43.
6. Ibid., 52.
7. Ibid., 54.
8. Michael Novak, *Will It Liberate? Questions About Liberation Theology* (New York: Paulist Press, 1986).
9. Michael Novak, *A Theology for Radical Politics* (New York: Herder & Herder, 1969), 122–28.
10. Gary Dorrien, *The Neoconservative Mind* (Philadelphia: Temple University Press, 1993), 207–64.

11. Novak, *The Catholic Ethic and the Spirit of Capitalism*. 126.
12. Richard John Neuhaus, "The Thorough Revolutionary," in Peter L. Berger and Richard John Neuhaus, *Movement and Revolution* (Garden City, N.Y.: Doubleday & Co., 1970), 127.
13. Peter L. Berger, quoted in Dorrien, *The Neoconservative Mind,* 322.
14. Richard John Neuhaus, *The Naked Public Square: Religion and Democracy in America* (Grand Rapids: Eerdmans, 1984).
15. James Davison Hunter, *Culture Wars: The Struggle to Define America* (New York: Basic Books, 1991), 57.
16. Ibid., 106.
17. Neuhaus, *The Naked Public Square,* 220.
18. Ibid., 69–73.
19. *Christianity and Democracy* (Washington, D.C.: Institute on Religion and Democracy, 1981), 5–6.
20. Ibid., 10–11.
21. "Ideology Under the Alms," *Newsweek,* February 3, 1983, 61.
22. Richard John Neuhaus, quoted in Howell, "Funding the War of Ideas" (see note 4 of chap 5). 44.
23. Richard John Neuhaus, "Democratic Conservatism," *First Things,* March 1990, 65.
24. Richard John Neuhaus, quoted in Howell, "Funding the War of Ideas," 43.
25. Ernest W. Lefever, *Amsterdam to Nairobi: The World Council of Churches and the Third World* (Washington, D.C.: Ethics and Public Policy Center, 1979).
26. Leon Howell, "Ernest Lefever at the Edge of Power: A Profile of Consistency," *Christianity and Crisis,* March 2, 1981, 41.
27. Ernest W. Lefever, *Nairobi to Vancouver: The World Council of Churches and the World, 1975–87* (Washington, D.C.: Ethics and Public Policy Center, 1987), 86, 89.
28. Howell, "Funding the War of Ideas," 1.
29. Leon Howell, "Funding the War of Ideas: The Role of the 'Four Sisters,' " *The Christian Century,* July 19–26, 1995, 701–2.
30. Ibid.

Chapter 8:
What Does a Good Ideology Require?

1. Joseph S. Roucek, *Social Control* (New York: D. Van Nostrand Company, 1947), 186.

Chapter 9:
Democratic Humanism: Toward a Convivial World

1. Mark Shields, "Pay the Workers," *The Washington Post,* August 22, 1995, A17.
2. Lester Thurow, *The Future of Capitalism* (New York: William Morrow, 1996), 257.

3. Ibid., 255.
4. Werner Sombart, quoted in Michael Harrington, *Socialism* (New York: Saturday Review Press, 1972), 109.
5. Barbara Crossette, "U.N. Study Finds a Free Eastern Europe Poorer and Less Healthy," *The New York Times,* October 7, 1994, A13.
6. R. H. Tawney, *Religion and the Rise of Capitalism* (New York: The New American Library, 1947), 235. Originally published in 1926.
7. John Kenneth Galbraith, *The Affluent Society* (Boston: Houghton Mifflin, 1958), 253.
8. Karl Polanyi, "The Role of Markets in Capitalist Society," in *The Capitalist System,* ed. Richard C. Edwards et al. (Englewood Cliffs, N.J.: Prentice-Hall, 1972), 95–96.
9. M. Douglas Meeks, *God the Economist: The Doctrine of God and Political Economy* (Minneapolis: Fortress Press, 1989). See esp. chaps. 2 and 3.
10. Polanyi, "The Role of Markets in Capitalist Society," 97.
11. Harrington, *Socialism,* 1–2.
12. E. J. Dionne, Jr., *They Only Look Dead: Why Progressives Will Dominate the Next Political Era* (New York: Simon & Schuster, 1996), 274.
13. Ralph Miliband, "The Socialist Alternative," in *Capitalism, Socialism, and Democracy Revisited,* ed. Larry Diamond and Marc F. Plattner (Baltimore: Johns Hopkins University Press, 1993), 113.
14. Thurow, *The Future of Capitalism,* 2, 21.
15. Shields, "Pay the Workers."
16. Thurow, *The Future of Capitalism,* 18.
17. A more detailed analysis of "The Seven Deadly D's" was provided in Alan Geyer, "America's Political Breakdown," *Christianity and Crisis,* March 2, 1992, 64–66.
18. Robert A. Dahl, "Why Free Markets Are Not Enough," in Diamond and Plattner, eds., *Capitalism, Socialism, and Democracy Revisited,* 81.
19. Thurow, *The Future of Capitalism,* 290–92.
20. Ibid., 305–6.
21. Francisco C. Weffort, "The Future of Socialism," in Diamond and Plattner, eds., *Capitalism, Socialism, and Democracy Revisited,* 92.
22. Robert N. Bellah et al., "Individualism and the Crisis of Civic Membership," *The Christian Century,* May 8, 1996, 514.
23. Ibid., 510–13.
24. Amitai Etzioni, *The Spirit of Community: Rights, Responsibilities, and the Communitarian Agenda* (New York: Crown Publishers, 1993), 247.
25. Walter G. Muelder, "Communitarian Christian Ethics: A Personal Statement and a Response," in *Toward a Discipline of Social Ethics: Essays in Honor of Walter George Muelder,* ed. Paul Deats, Jr. (Boston: Boston University Press, 1972), 295–320.
26. Gary Dorrien, *The Democratic Socialist Vision* (Totowa, N.J.: Rowman & Littlefield, 1986) and *Reconstructing the Common Good: Theology and the Social Order* (Maryknoll, N.Y.: Orbis Books, 1990).

27. Dean Button, "It's the System," an interview with Gar Alperovitz, *Ecological Economics Bulletin,* April 1996, 4–10.
28. John B. Cobb, Jr., *Sustaining the Common Good: A Christian Perspective on the Global Economy* (Cleveland: Pilgrim Press, 1994), 45–46.
29. Ibid., 124.
30. John D. Deardourff, "Guarantees for Children," *The Washington Post,* June 9, 1996, C7.
31. Alan Geyer, "Toward a Convivial Theology," *The Christian Century,* April 23, 1969, 541–44.
32. Ivan Illich, *Tools for Conviviality* (New York: Harper & Row, 1973).
33. Reinhold Niebuhr, *The Children of Light and the Children of Darkness* (New York: Charles Scribner's Sons, 1944), xi.
34. Ibid., 151.
35. Walter Rauschenbusch, *Christianizing the Social Order* (New York: Macmillan Co., 1912), 353, 361.
36. Various approaches to economic democracy are discussed in Linda J. Medcalf and Kenneth M. Dolbeare, *Neopolitics: American Political Ideas in the 1980s* (New York: Random House, 1985), esp. chap. 6, "Economic Democracy: Democratic Neopopulism."
37. Beverly Harrison, *Making the Connections* (Boston: Beacon Press, 1985), 72.
38. Frank Freidel, *Franklin D. Roosevelt: A Rendezvous with Destiny* (Boston: Little, Brown & Co., 1990), 500.
39. Martin Carnoy, Derek Shearer, and Russell Rumberger, *A New Social Contract: The Economy and Government After Reagan* (New York: Harper & Row, 1983), 230. Cited in Medcalf and Dolbeare, *Neopolitics,* 101.
40. National Conference of Catholic Bishops, *Economic Justice for All: Catholic Social Teaching and the U.S. Economy* (Washington, D.C.: U.S. Catholic Conference, 1986), 41.
41. Ibid., 49.
42. Audrey Chapman Smock, ed., *Christian Faith and Economic Life* (New York: United Church Board for World Ministries, 1987).
43. Walter Brueggemann, Sharon Parks, and Thomas H. Groome, *To Act Justly, Love Tenderly, Walk Humbly* (Mahwah, N.J.: Paulist Press, 1986), 16.
44. E. J. Dionne, Jr., "Muddying the Waters with Facts," *The Washington Post,* May 28, 1996, A–11.
45. James A. Nash, "On the Goodness of Government," *Theology and Public Policy,* Winter 1995, 3.
46. Stephen L. Elkin, "PEGS and Wholes," *The Good Society,* Fall 1995, 13. (PEGS refers to the Committee on the Political Economy of the Good Society.)
47. Dionne, *They Only Look Dead,* 286, 313.

Chapter 10:
Political Ecclesiology: Toward a Convivial Church

1. Clarence True Wilson, quoted in George Mecklenburg, *Bowing the Preacher Out of Politics* (New York: Fleming H. Revell Co., 1928), 19. Other sources

for political hermeneutics include Oscar Cullmann, *The State in the New Testament* (New York: Charles Scribner's Sons, 1955); John Howard Yoder, *The Politics of Jesus* (Grand Rapids: Eerdmans, 1972); Norman K. Gottwald and Richard Horsley, eds., *The Bible and Liberation: Political and Social Hermeneutics* (Maryknoll, N.Y.: Orbis Books, 1983, 1993); Richard Bauckham, *The Bible in Politics: How to Read the Bible Politically* (Louisville: Westminster/John Knox Press, 1989); David Jobling et al., eds., *The Bible and the Politics of Exegesis* (Cleveland: Pilgrim Press, 1991).

2. Joseph L. Allen, *Love and Conflict: A Covenantal Model of Christian Ethics* (Nashville: Abingdon Press, 1984), 289–91.

3. Gustavo Gutiérrez, *A Theology of Liberation* (Maryknoll, N.Y.: Orbis Books, 1973), 12–13.

4. Alan Geyer, *Piety and Politics: American Protestantism in the World Arena* (Richmond: John Knox Press, 1963), 103.

5. H. Mark Roelofs' description of "the Protestant/Bourgeois Complex" is summarized in chapter 4 of this book.

6. Brooks Hays, *Politics Is My Parish* (Baton Rouge, La.: Louisiana State University Press, 1981), 47.

7. Johannes Christiaan Hoekendijk, *The Church Inside Out* (Philadelphia: Westminster Press, 1966).

8. World Council of Churches, *The Church for Others* (Geneva: World Council of Churches, 1967), 18.

9. These lines are from the fourth verse of the hymn, "O Brother Man, Fold to Thy Heart Thy Brother," by John Greenleaf Whittier, *The Methodist Hymnal* (Nashville: The Methodist Publishing House, 1996), 199.

INDEX

INDEX